To Julie
with gratitude
Maxine x

'The Ripple Effect' Process

AN INTRODUCTION TO
PSYCHO-EMOTIONAL-EDUCATION

Maxine Harley

BALBOA
PRESS
A DIVISION OF HAY HOUSE

Copyright © 2012 Maxine Harley

All rights reserved. No part of this book may be used or reproduced by any means, graphic, electronic, or mechanical, including photocopying, recording, taping or by any information storage retrieval system without the written permission of the publisher except in the case of brief quotations embodied in critical articles and reviews.

ISBN: 978-1-4525-5664-2 (sc)
ISBN: 978-1-4525-5678-9 (e)
ISBN: 978-1-4525-5665-9 (hc)

Balboa Press books may be ordered through booksellers or by contacting:

Balboa Press
A Division of Hay House
1663 Liberty Drive
Bloomington, IN 47403
www.balboapress.com
1-(877) 407-4847

Because of the dynamic nature of the Internet, any web addresses or links contained in this book may have changed since publication and may no longer be valid. The views expressed in this work are solely those of the author and do not necessarily reflect the views of the publisher, and the publisher hereby disclaims any responsibility for them.

The author of this book does not dispense medical advice or prescribe the use of any technique as a form of treatment for physical, emotional, or medical problems without the advice of a physician, either directly or indirectly. The intent of the author is only to offer information of a general nature to help you in your quest for emotional and spiritual well-being. In the event you use any of the information in this book for yourself, which is your constitutional right, the author and the publisher assume no responsibility for your actions.

Any people depicted in stock imagery provided by Thinkstock are models, and such images are being used for illustrative purposes only.
Certain stock imagery © Thinkstock.

Printed in the United States of America

Balboa Press rev. date: 08/28/2012

Preface

I used to find life hard. For too many years I'd tried to get it right, but I just kept on tripping myself up and falling into the gaps that existed in my own life. I'd climb back out, dust myself down, pretend I didn't feel ashamed, paint on my confident face and set out again, only to keep repeating the same process. I just didn't have the map which would show me how to reach a happy and worthwhile life; but I did have an inkling that such a map existed, at least metaphorically, although I suspected that it was only available to people who'd had a much different background to me, and that if by chance I ever did get to see such a map then I wouldn't be able to understand it, let alone use it properly anyway. This book illuminates and reflects my own arduous trek to create such a map which shows the way towards a better life—for those of us who need a bit of help and guidance along the way. A map which can be used by anyone willing to get their sturdy boots on and undertake the journey to a life without the big gaps into which they have also been falling.

I will begin by explaining the 'why and what' reasons for my writing this book. The 'why' stems from my growing awareness of a need for something new which can fill in the gaps—more gaps!—that still exist in current therapeutic services and in what they have to offer to the public. The 'what' is an introduction to 'The Ripple Effect' Process, a programme of psycho-emotional-education which I have created as a new approach to overall emotional and psychological well-being. I don't intend this book to just be a marketing tool—

that would be selfish, inconsiderate and arrogant of me to say the least—and so I have been sure to include insights, tips, expanded information, and even a few poems and visualisations which I hope will make the whole book more comprehensive, informative, relevant and attractive to you. I want it to be the sort of book that you will happily pass on to someone else, or even encourage them to have their own copy to use and refer to themselves.

Over recent years the phrase 'ripple effect' frequently arose in my work as a psychotherapist. I would often hear myself use the term to describe the effects that even a simple change in ourselves can have upon the wider world. We are all energy in a bigger field of energy, and everything has an effect upon everything else. I know first-hand that significant personal change is possible as I myself have changed considerably since being the angry, aggressive and neurotic young woman that I once was. My own life path has meandered along with its own twists and turns, steep climbs and sharp drops, and I can hardly recognise the person I used to be—although I do feel sympathy for her struggle, and gratitude for her persistence. My own path to growth and change has had a ripple effect upon my relationships with my daughter and grandson; and with my more recent choice of friends, as well as with the clients I have had the privilege of working with over the last 17 years. I have often seen this ripple effect of change in my clients' daily lives too, and in the ways in which they have improved their own relationships, particularly with their partners and children, and most importantly with themselves. The name for this new form of therapeutic help therefore had to be 'The Ripple Effect'!

In creating the twelve modules of 'The Ripple Effect' Process, my aim has been to de-mystify therapy, and to make known to the general public information, skills and theories usually held 'close to the chest' of those individuals earning lots of money in the areas of psychological and emotional well-being. Over the last 25 years I have studied not only counselling and psychotherapy, but also energy psychology, functional/natural medicine, nutrition, meditation and its effects upon the brain, and many other aspects of neuroscience. Such has been my quest for my own map! I have now combined relevant and significant aspects of my knowledge of the many traditional therapeutic approaches, skills and theories used by the wide variety of professional therapists, with more up-to-date research-based information, skills-training, and contemporary holistic lifestyle ideas. I have also included new and crucial information which has recently become known from the neuro-scientific research into brain development and how this affects our behaviours. I have added the vital ingredients of nutrition, natural remedies, self-help life-enhancing activities, attentive awareness, and meditation. This integration makes the programme of 'The Ripple Effect' Process a comprehensive, relevant, and effective method of attaining psychological, emotional, and consequently spiritual well-being. So it has become a three dimensional map with its own contours and textures.

All counsellors and psychotherapists will have undergone any one of the vast array of different types of training on offer. Each training course having its own levels of academic and experiential input, and different standards and levels of qualifications. Having completed their training these therapists will have had the 'heirloom' of their particular chosen method of therapy passed down to them, for them to replicate and 'make-fit' with the clients with whom they then work, whether in a paid or voluntary setting. One size does not fit all however, and over the last twenty years or so, there has been a growing awareness of this, leading to a blending and eclectic mixing of the different approaches to counselling and psychotherapy. The work of Thomas Leonard in the 1990's added to the mix with the introduction of coaching training and the quickly emerging professions of 'life-coach' and 'business-coach'.

All of the existing approaches to therapy focus upon the aspect of the individual that they consider to be at the core of the difficulties the client experiences in their life. These different approaches include styles of psychotherapy called Cognitive-Behavioural, Person-Centred, Existential, Trans-personal, Solution-focussed, Gestalt, Transactional Analysis, Jungian, Psychodynamic, Bodywork,

Sensory-Motor, Psychoanalytical, Rational-Emotive, and several other offshoots of these. However, research has shown that it is the therapeutic relationship, as well as the optimism of the client and their readiness for help, that determines how effective they consider their experience of counselling therapy to have been, and not the particular theoretical approach used. We are all much more than simply our thoughts, or our feelings, or our bodily sensations and awareness, or our dreams, or our history; we are all unique and much more complex than any one approach allows for, or has the remit to provide help for. After twenty years of learning about the many different theories and styles of working, as well as having my own base of integrative counselling and psychotherapy training, I have become acutely aware of the short-comings of these differing approaches, and of some of their proponents. It became apparent to me from the many clients I had worked with, either individually or as a couple or group, that there needed to be something new that filled in the professional gaps and provided a more relevant and comprehensive way of helping people to change. Many existing approaches do not even offer the prospect of change!

Unlike many other professions or trades, the work of counsellors, coaches and psychotherapists cannot be seen and quantified, and any personal changes experienced by a client are anecdotal and subjective in nature. We engage a therapist because we want to feel better, we want our life to change in some significant way, we want to be understood and accepted by someone who has the qualifications, skills and experience to guide us, and who can also keep us emotionally supported during this process.

I have attended many conferences, seminars, workshops and lectures including some from the 'experts' in the field of psychotherapy. I have seen how they work and I have read their books, and hundreds more. I realised many years ago that the base-line 'way of being with a client'—of showing them empathy, interest, attention and validation—were not in themselves a sufficient agent of change—despite being an invaluable way of connecting with someone on a deeper emotional level. Just talking about your difficulties over weeks, months, or even years, does not guarantee that things will change for you. It will only ensure that you have a story to tell about your problems, struggles and shortcomings. Certain therapeutic approaches assume that the client will simply find their own way through their maze of conflicting thoughts and experiences, without ever having been taught how to do so. Having someone reflect back to you, paraphrasing and summarising, what you have just said, or even asking you open-ended questions (designed to get you to expand your awareness of your problem), may be helpful in certain chaotic circumstances—but these are not enough to bring about tangible changes in your life, despite the time and money involved in this type of counselling. Conversely, choosing a solution/cognitively-focussed 'common-sense' approach to re-framing your problems, doesn't reach your deeper experiences and ingrained emotional responses that have created the difficulties that you are seeking help for.

Therapy is a professional relationship which includes payment for a 'service'. I have heard this referred to as being like an emotional prostitute, paid by a client to attune to their emotional and psychological needs, helping them to offload and have relief from their problems. There is never a full and mutual relationship with a client because of ethical professional boundaries, although I have genuinely cared about them all, and on occasions have made that known. I wanted to give my clients more than just my time, attention and care, or my ability to ask various types of effective questions. I wanted them to have something of longer-term use and value to take away from our sessions. I wanted them to get what they were paying for. Despite the way of working modelled by the eminent therapists I had paid to witness, I would keep returning to my favoured position of introducing an explanation, or a diagram, or an exercise of some sort. All of which were intended to expand my client's personal insight and awareness, and to access areas not reached by mainstream methods. The feedback I had from these methods showed me that this openness was appreciated and very useful, and I have regularly included it whenever I felt that the particular needs of a client invited it. When we have the opportunity to learn more about who we really are—and why—and about our emotions and moods, and how to change them; and we learn too about many other important aspects of how to live a more balanced and meaningful life, then this will have a profound effect upon the people we have contact with....and so the ripple effect slowly expands outwards into the world. The twelve modules of 'The Ripple Effect' Process are available to all adults who are able to make use of them, and I am particularly keen to attract mothers and mothers-to-be onto the modules, because the changes that each woman makes within herself, as she becomes more knowledgeable, more emotionally balanced, and a wiser mother and guide to her own child(ren), will then ripple down to the next generation.

I will begin in Part One of this book by looking at the 'Gaps': both the gaps we all have in our individual sense of ourselves and our lives, and the gaps in what is on offer from the professional services. The modules of 'The Ripple Effect' Process are carefully designed to help to fill in these gaps. I will then share with you, in Part Two, how I set up the whole project, including my own stumbling and learning along the way. Following this, in Part Three, I will say something about each of the twelve topics that make up the modules of 'The Ripple Effect' Process. These modules are already being presented by authorised licensees around the country who have previously had their own type of therapeutic training, and who are working with the public in their own private practices. Each module, whether one of the six four-hour workshops, or one of the six eight-week groups, is offered to small groups of up to six people. Attending one of these modules is a much richer and deeper experience than can be shown in the overview presented here. If I were to include the actual content of each module here that would take up far too much space—and would be the equivalent of another two books! There is also the possibility that you might try and use them as a short-cut to actually being in a small group and being part of that richer experience—which would then rob you of your fuller potential for learning, sharing and change. Alas, there is also the risk that an unscrupulous person might try and throw together workshops or ongoing groups of their own from any expanded disclosure of the content of the modules. Whilst not wishing to sound paranoid, human nature shows that this is unfortunately a distinct possibility. I will however offer you something here which I hope will be of use to you just from reading this book. I'll also give you a flavour of each module, and what it has to offer, should you wish to attend it. In Part Four I have included plenty of extra material for you which is not included in 'The Ripple Effect' Process. This is in the form of 36 articles I have recently written, plus some shorter snippets, and 12 visualisations for you to use.

The ripple is a symbol of growth, sharing, hope, and change. We are all energy and as such we all affect one another in many unseen ways. When we refine and clarify what we intend to project out into the world we give the best of ourselves for others, who are in turn affected by that and undergo changes in themselves too.

I am someone who never believed that she could write a book—but here I am on an incongruously snowy day in April starting to do just that! I have changed so much myself, and I now know that great change is possible given the right opportunity, guidance, direction, and support. I sincerely hope that the modules of 'The Ripple Effect' Process will provide these conditions for your own growth and change, so that you can fill in and heal the gaps that have been tripping you up and getting in the way of you being all that you deserve to be.

The Gaps

Personal Gaps

Once when I accompanied my daughter to view a house that she wanted to live in, I was shocked and dismayed to find out—the hard way—that a large gap in the main bedroom floorboards was covered up with a rug, which did nothing to fill the gap in the floor or prevent the almost inevitable accident. This image has stayed with me and I think it makes a useful analogy here.

If we each think in terms of our own self and psyche being like a house, then the deficits, mistakes and oversights in the construction will inevitably show themselves, if not immediately then over time. Profound faults will make the house have less commercial value, and such a fix-up project should only be taken on by someone skilled and proficient with such work and the personal costs involved. It might however be attempted by someone who was well-intentioned but naïve in the realm of property repairs, renovations and refurbishments, and who might pour their time, effort and money into the project, yet never reap the desired results and rewards.

I have in the past actually renovated a few houses—as well as taken on too many relationship projects requiring a great amount of time and effort in trying to achieve the 'potential' that I saw for the finished product. I have wasted many years and spent a great deal of money patiently, yet fruitlessly, trying to fill a bottomless pit of faults, in both properties and relationships, that were profound structural faults, and not, as I'd naively thought, purely cosmetic in nature.

The rug may be expensive and attractive, but the gaps in the floorboards still lie hidden beneath, and will trip the unsuspecting guest. The picture on the wall may be skewed off-centre, or perhaps be part of a large group of pictures, the aim of which appears to be the offering to the observer of a scene of beauty and interest; but their real purpose is to hide ugly cracks in the wall behind them. The wallpaper may be richly coloured and textured to distract from the cracks and gaps which have been cheaply and temporarily filled beneath it. The house may have 'kerb appeal' and be attractive to the eye from the distance of the roadside, with its newly painted picket fence and colourfully planted tubs and borders; the grass may have been cut, the porch de-cluttered, and the doorstep washed, but behind the pretty facade lies only an empty and barren structure rather than a welcoming home. The appealing and seductive frontage promises so much more than the neglected interior can deliver. A prospective owner probably wouldn't think to turn on the taps, and check the water flow and pressure; but if they did they would soon realise that the boiler and plumbing system was in need of major repair and updating. Neither would they notice, in their enthusiasm for the project ahead, that the windows were ill-fitting and draughty, and that there were damp patches in several hard-to-see places. The urgent need for underpinning of the foundations may have been deliberately obscured due to the fear of exposing the full extent of the subsidence. But some flaws cannot be hidden under the carpet or concealed by carefully placed pictures or furniture. When the joists are rotten they must be replaced. When our sense of self and our psyche is riddled with emotional woodworm it will collapse under pressure.

We've all got gaps. Gaps in our sense of who we are, in our integrity, in our personality and in our character. Some of us also have gaps in our ability to relate in a comfortable and rewarding way with other people; gaps in our authenticity, and the ease with which we can be genuine, playful and spontaneous; and gaps in our connection to where we have come from and where we are going to in our lives. Most of us have gaps in our empathy and compassion for the vulnerable child we once were—a child who was doing the best he or she could to stay alive, and to be liked by, and useful to, other people.

If you are really lucky your gaps will only be hairline cracks; because you were a wanted and loved child. Because your parents, or other caretakers, gave you the time, interest and attention that made you feel like you mattered to them. Because they were fair and clear and consistent in both their treatment of you, and the dialogue they had with you. Because they listened to you with genuine concern. Because they did all that they could to make your life as interesting, rewarding and meaningful as was possible. They treated you as the special gift that you truly were, but without overindulging or overprotecting you.

There is no such thing as a perfect childhood or a perfect parent. We can only hope that any child's experiences are good-enough that they are left feeling secure in who they are, and in what they can accomplish in their life. However having a good-enough childhood is still no guarantee that you will sail through life unhindered. You may not have had to develop the resources needed to be able to weather the storms that life will inevitably throw at you....and you too will therefore have your own gaps.

For those of us whose childhood and family experiences were very different from those good-enough ones described above……we are left with bigger gaps. Sometimes they are so big that no matter how hard we try to ignore them or convince other people that they don't exist, we keep falling into them, and painfully exposing our hidden shame. This is particularly painful when we have sabotaged our own success and happiness, or when alcohol knocks out our desperately needed inhibitors, allowing our flawed and damaged selves to show up and ruin things in a whole myriad of ways. We can be as creative in our own downfall and demise as we are in creating a convincing facade. A facade which was created and designed to fool people into believing that we don't have any of the gaps that we try so hard to keep hidden from view. We dread exposure. We are paralysed by the potential of shame to kick our legs from under us and to prove to the world just how imperfect we really are.

The inadequate parenting which causes our gaps is not always obvious to the outside world. If a mother doesn't bond with her baby, then that child won't feel loved, wanted and valued, and more significantly it won't have the enormous benefits to its emotional and physical health that Oxytocin—called the 'cuddle and bonding hormone'—would otherwise bring. Lack of Oxytocin is implicated in a wide array of psychological problems, or as we are calling them here, 'gaps', as well as in mental ill-health too. If you grew up in a house overcast by tension, arguments and a hostile atmosphere created by parents who didn't want to be together, or who were preoccupied with their own traumas and emotional and/or physical pain, and unmet needs; or if you grew up in a house with lots of siblings or other family members all creating their own noise and vying to get their needs met, then you too will have gaps because you will not have had the time, attention and care that you really needed as a child. If a parent, who perhaps feels the shame of not having amounted to much themselves—or maybe they were talented in some way and did achieve a level of success and notoriety—directs their child's life into one of achievement, and expects nothing less than perfection from that child, then the child will develop gaps in their own sense of identity and in their personal feelings of worthiness—which they will believe to be conditional upon their achievements, success and parental approval. If a parent is narcissistic or attention-seeking and 'steals the show' they then leave the child waiting in the shadows of their life; or if a parent was unable to regulate their own emotions and moods, or was chaotic, unpredictable or even frightening; or if a parent needed their child to take the place of a lost sibling, absent partner or longed-for best friend and confidante, than that child will grow up to have gaps. If a child has to play out a role in order to keep up the family image, such as being the bad/mad/sick one, or the happy and grateful offspring, then that child will have gaps too. If a child has too much responsibility put on their shoulders such as having to look after younger siblings or a long-term sick, or mentally-ill, or substance-abusing parent, and so misses out on vital parts of their own childhood and peer relationships; or if a child is either the 'favoured/special/chosen' one, or they can see and feel that a sibling has been favoured above them—then, yes you've guessed it—they'll have gaps too. As will a child brought up by someone other than the woman in whose womb he/she was created and first bonded with. That may be due to a mother having died; or because a busy professional family employ nannies to do the care-taking for them; or a single mum who's busy doing two jobs and leaves the raising of a child in the ill-equipped hands of an older sibling; or, of course, if a child is adopted, or is sent to a boarding school at an early age—particularly if that was an abusive experience as it all too often is; or if the child is hospitalised for long periods away from home and from their mother or other loving care-giver.

If a child is humiliated, ridiculed, shamed, beaten, neglected, ignored, traumatised or abused in any way, then the gaps will be wider and deeper. They will ache and bleed, they remain raw and sore. All attempts at covering them up are futile….you still have the gaps and they won't go away. They determine the path that you stumble along every day of your difficult life.

There are now even Diagnostic and Statistical manuals available in the professional therapy sector, which categorise the way in which the gaps show themselves in our lives—in the form of neurotic behaviours, personality disorders (which most people can be said to have to a certain degree anyway) and some forms of mental illness associated with a lack of attachment to a secure and nurturing person in our early developmental years.

In highlighting my own gaps I want to make clear that this is not going to become another memoir of a wounded and hated child. Sadly there are too many of us around. I am not a competent storyteller anyway. I was never given the opportunity to talk about myself as a child—something referred to in psychotherapy circles as 'developing a personal narrative'—and so I did not know how to do so. My secret pain and imaginary dialogues had to stay safely inside of me, where they steadily accumulated, gaining weight and pressure, until they felt like they might at any moment burst forth in a torrent of despair and disclosure to someone, anyone, who just might show me an inkling of interest, kindness, care or concern. That didn't happen, and it would have been much too painful if it had. This, in psycho-speak, is called the 'juxtaposition', of dreading and avoiding the very help and care that you know deep down that you want and need the most, because to receive it would be much too painful. I did not, at the time, tell anyone the story of the slaps, thumps, kicks, bruises, knife attacks, humiliation, shame, or the erratic and sexually confusing boundaries in my own childhood. I believed that no-one would have listened to me anyway, and that I would have somehow been seriously punished for sharing what goes on 'behind closed doors' if they had. I can't and don't talk of this early part of my life in any detail. It all had to become a blur in order for me to remain strong in my hatred of my parents—that word 'parent' just doesn't seem to fit, and I feel awkward writing the word, but that is what they should have been at least. The heat and strength of this hatred fuelled my yearning to escape, and to find a sanctuary. Had I not kept myself fired up with rage and hatred I feared that I might sink into the hopeless place of a passive and helpless victim resigned to my fate. I could never do that. I waited for rescue. I was sure that Social Services would come one day and take me to a better place—how naïve I was. I had a fantasy that I had been given to the wrong family by the maternity hospital and that one day the mistake would be uncovered and my real and loving parents would turn up out of the blue and reclaim me—and punish the people I had been forced to live with until then, for their neglect and cruelty towards me. This fantasy was kept alive in my mind, body and soul for years, more so because I did not physically resemble other members of my family. Rescue never came, and by the time I reached my teenage years I finally gave up the hope and fantasy that it would come, in any form. I would just have to keep on waiting until I was old enough to leave. My mother, as I shall call her here, even gave me a suitcase. I don't recall her giving me any other gifts. I left as soon as I could. The gaps of the parents become the gaps of the children.

I still have gaps. I hate those gaps and yet I owe them so much too. Without my gaps, and my awareness of them, and my relentless quest to fill them, you would not be reading this book, because I would have had a happier life and a different path. I don't need to tell you my story. You have your own story and some of what I am saying may resonate with you and your story too.

I envy people who can tell an engaging account of their holidays or family events with such detail, texture and colour that the listener almost shares the experience with them. I would never have believed that one day I would even consider writing a book! There were no books in our house, and I read as little as I could get away with at school. Yet I have, over the last 20 years or so, read hundreds books associated with therapy, personal and spiritual development and healthy living. I have been ravenous for knowledge about the subjects that resonate with me. I am now hearing the voice in my head that tells me that this book won't be worth the time and effort of writing it anyway. That people like me don't write books; and that no-one will even be interested in my opinions, my ideas and what I have to say. I have now learned that this doubt-inducing and mocking voice really has my best interests at heart—it is just out-of-date. It tries to ensure that I avoid potentially shaming and humiliating situations and their consequences. It is trying to keep me safe. I appreciate that, and although I hear the words of doubt and the attempts at sabotage, I no longer permit them the power to stop me from expressing myself. At least not in writing. I haven't yet mastered the internal voices that can literally take away my own voice if I should attempt to speak in front of a group of people, but I'm working on that challenge!

On reflection I could not have chosen a better childhood experience to get me to where I am now. My painful experiences set me up for further ones that reinforced them, and which then ensured that a self-fulfilling prophecy continued to play out and to hold me in its grasp. Whilst I struggled and lived in fear—often for my life—I could not have realised that those very experiences would, or could, have a positive outcome. Had my life been worse I would have unravelled and may have taken the route into self-harm and substance abuse; but thankfully I didn't. As a teenager I often wondered why I had not become a drug-taker, or a prostitute or a criminal......the foundations for such a life were in place for me. Something higher than my limited day to day awareness clearly had a different path in line for me to take. Like so many other people I drank too much in my teens and twenties—and again in my mid-40's when my daughter had grown up and I was 'free' to play again, after all the years of struggling emotionally, physically and financially as a single parent. I assured attention from men at that time by the sexy way in which I dressed. I liked how witty and carefree I became after only a couple of glasses of wine......which always led to too much more, and then to the wasting of the next day trapped in the headlock of the inevitable punishing hangover. I was vulnerable when drunk and unfortunately there have been men who have taken advantage of this—they also had gaps which they tried to fill in their own ways. I would often cry alone after these so-called fun encounters when the bitter pain of emptiness, loneliness and despair inevitably replaced the distraction that the alcohol-induced games had temporarily given me.

If I were to 'assess' my former self from my present-day professional perspective, I would say that I had a lack of Oxytocin due to being an unwanted, neglected and hated child—brought up by parents who themselves had unresolved traumas and who both also would have had low Oxytocin and Beta-Endorphin levels due to the inadequate parenting they had each received; and that their loveless marriage created bitterness, resentment and violence which affected the children—who were an unwanted burden. I would have to add to this 'diagnosis' that I had developed an insecure 'attachment style' which led me to distrust and avoid emotionally intimate people and relationships. I would also say that I had little self-esteem which I compensated for by being funny, sexy or aggressive, and that my significant emotional and physical traumas were unresolved and therefore caused me difficulties in balancing and calming my own emotional state, resulting in temporary dysfunctional mood-enhancing behaviours. Hmmm......it all sounds so clear and straightforward from my present-day 'informed' standpoint. If only I'd known all of this years ago I could have tried to find the help and guidance I needed. Conversely, had my childhood and later experiences been much more positive I am sure that I would not have become a psychotherapist, or have created 'The Ripple Effect' Process (or the Quantum Psyche Process—which is the subject of my next book).

I do wonder how differently I would feel inside if I had been loved as a child. I will never know, but I do wonder. I imagine I would feel more whole, connected, complete, secure in who I am, more grounded, and somehow just 'better' than I am. Instead I have always felt—deep inside and hidden from view—like a cautious kitten cowering in a corner, or under the sofa, waiting, waiting, waiting, for the threat to go away. Ready to spit, hiss and scratch if anyone came too close too quickly. Like any child with big gaps in who they are, I developed emotional antennae, which were sensitively attuned to any changes in the mood and atmosphere around me. These have served me well, but at a cost. They were meant to keep me safe from pain, but yet they were so alert to even the possibility of pain, that I then avoided any potential opportunities for love—which I couldn't even recognise, let alone believe in. I avoided good, kind and loving people because I thought them strange and not to be trusted. If I let my guard down they could hurt me more deeply than anyone would imagine I could be hurt; and so I stayed safe but isolated. My antennae have since served as a vital asset to me as a psychotherapist working with the damage and wounds of my clients. I have been able to pick up the slight nuances that accompany a painful, hidden or repressed memory. My emotional antennae have helped me to genuinely empathise with clients far beyond the 'skills' taught in my counselling training years ago.

My own gap-filling, which is an ongoing process, has enabled me to be with someone else's pain and distress, and to have a deeper heartfelt knowing of their soul's angst, rather than merely a superficial sympathy, or an imagining of what it must have been like to have had their experiences. Clearly there are many experiences that I have not had personally, but those I have are wide-ranging and they have informed me a great deal both as a foster-carer and as a counsellor, psychotherapist and kinesiologist.

As a foster-carer for 'hard-to-place' teenage girls—which ironically I would have been myself many years earlier had I been rescued by Social Services—I have often witnessed their relief when I've said that it is understandable that they don't love their parent(s) and that some parents behave so badly, usually without fully realising the full extent of what they are doing, that it is very difficult to even like them, let alone to love them. This would often contrast with what they were being told, from well-meaning social workers, at the time. Yes, ideally we should love our parents, but telling a child with big gaps, where love is absent and bleeding scars exist, that they should love their abusive parents is only imposing conditions that ensure a lack of congruence and authenticity in the child. The child knows and feels what they know and feel; and the professional adults, however well-intentioned should not try to mould a child or young person into something which feels false and alien to them—even if it is 'office policy and procedure'!

In my psychotherapy work several clients have said to me, after our therapy contract had ended, that they had for some unknown reason felt particularly drawn to working with me rather than one of the many other therapists available. They said too that they had a feeling that I really knew their experience because they imagined that I'd had something similar enough happen to me in my life. They would add that this had really helped them to feel courageous enough to share their pain and shame, and to continue with the difficult journey of healing their own wounds, and of becoming a thriver instead of just a survivor. Sharing of similar experiences links us in a unique way. We have a trust and respect for the inner strength, resilience and resourcefulness of one another. It is strange and yet wonderful that we know, on some deeper or higher level, what and whom we most need to guide us along our individual path. Friends have asked me how I've managed to work with the deeply emotional and disturbing issues that clients bring into therapy. I believe that my own gaps have actually served me well here, because I have been able to be present with each person and to hear their often terrible story, and yet still remain emotionally self-contained. I am not like a sponge that soaks up other people's distress. If I were I would not be suited to such work. I am concerned and committed to helping in any way I can but I cannot take-on-board other people's emotions. I must maintain my own personal, and professional boundaries. My gaps have helped me to do this. I embarked upon a career in counselling and psychotherapy from the desire to help even one person to improve their life and for them to not thoughtlessly harm another person—particularly a child. If I have done so, and I know that I have, then the years of effort and expense have all been worthwhile. My own gaps will have been of service to another—and that then gives them value.

My own life experiences are, probably like yours, quite broad, and include those I have had thrust upon me as well as others I have chosen. Those which were out of my control include feeling like an unwelcome guest and the outcast in the family; having several car accidents—before the age of five years in my case (I was often told to "go and play with the traffic" and it seems that is literally what I did, with dangerous results due to the lack of any adult supervision or care). I also have gaps caused by being physically and emotionally neglected; physically and emotionally beaten; from overhearing my mother tell my father how much she hated me and that they would be better off without me around, and that she wished I'd never been born and that I would now just die; from my mother's jealousy and her violent attacks upon me; beatings from my father's fists and his leather belt; from bereavements; bullying; fear of death; rape; sexual assaults; alcohol poisoning; homelessness; large debts; abortion; single parenthood and struggling to exist on state benefits; cosmetic surgery—to reshape my nose which had been broken on more than one occasion; being sexually harassed; being on the receiving end of racism—whilst staying in a predominantly Aboriginal community in Australia several years ago; witnessing mob violence, murder and attempted murders. There are more, but I'm sure you get the point I am making. Which is that it is not so much any actual experience, but the sense we make of it, and the extent to which we allow it to negatively affect our own lives, and perhaps in turn, the lives of others we are in close contact with, that is important. The challenges I have chosen have been those which forced me to stand up tall in the face of my fears. I have walked on hot coals at an Anthony Robbins marathon weekend workshop (which probably now accounts for my chronic dislike of 'high-fives' and 'whoop-whoop'!); I have handled snakes and a tarantula, I have been scuba diving, water ski-ing, windsurfing, para-sailing and white water rafting (I wasn't any good at any of them but that doesn't matter) as a way of overcoming my fear of drowning—I nearly drowned when I was a small child; and I have abseiled and been rock climbing too. Goodbye energy-draining fear!

There can be negative ripple effects in life too. I can see that my own grandparents all had difficulties in their own lives, which were devoid of love and rife with shame, cruelty and struggles. They passed on to their children what they knew—the same way of life—albeit probably not as bad as they had experienced themselves, and so they thought they'd done a good job of parenting. My own paternal grandparents were both illegitimate—which would have been hugely shameful in those days. They found each other, which in itself is surprising, and had seven children—none of whom knew what a loving family was like and could therefore not pass this on to any of their fifteen offspring. And so the ripples grow—either negatively or positively. Fortunately the negative ripples can now be changed and gaps can be filled and healed in ways that were not available to our ancestors.

Those of us with the big gaps can be keenly aware of one another, if we allow ourselves to tune-in. Being confronted by the very gaps in someone else that you are trying hard to disguise or deny in yourself, can be very unsettling and you may instead just avoid one another The first signs of the gaps are what I call the 'BLAB' the 'body-language and boundaries'—which will either be too rigid, and hold the body in an aloof stiffness as if the other were in some way contaminated; or they may instead be too loose, with a body that gets too close to the other, invading the personal zone and touching the other person, as if by accident—as their inner child tentatively tries to reach out and connect, hoping to be liked and accepted by the other. The speech pattern is another give-away. It may be stilted, staccato, and sprinkled with mispronunciations—

paradoxically caused by the very act of trying too hard to get it right and not to make a mistake. Sarcastic and caustic comments may be exchanged in a banter to determine supremacy—a mutual antler tapping to see who is the most vulnerable and who is the emotionally tougher. Swear words might fill the gaps of a sentence instead of an adjective or pro-noun—these being the habits picked up from their parent-with-big-gaps. Overly flirtatious and sexually suggestive comments and body-language reveal a history of objectification and sexualisation. Any attempts at challenging such behaviour will be robustly defended and they will have a well-used adeptness at convincing the challenger that they are mistaken and have misinterpreted the behaviour and thereby caused offence by even suggesting such a thing had happened. If that fails and the dreaded shame is exposed then there will follow a punishing counter-shaming to even the score. Another indicator is when verbal silences are filled with trivia—anything to avoid an agonizing silence that might have allowed a negative evaluation and judgement to percolate.

When people with big gaps meet one another they can sniff the all-too-familiar fear that runs like a turbulent stream through every cell of the body. Only we can really know and empathise with the gnawing anxiety that bites at the gut and stabs every fibre of our being from the dawning of each new day. We feel the scrutiny of the other's eyes as we scan one another for any sign of threat. We may see in the other the submissive and downcast look of the silent victim—their apology for continuing to exist in the world. Or we feel their anger, and see the threat of aggression in their faces—which isn't convincingly covered over by a forced and misshapen smile which never reaches their eyes. No matter if we meet at a social or professional function, we can 'see' into the wounded soul of the other. There is a shared knowing that comes from the fear and struggle we have each had in our own past. We are all running on fear—it is the fuel that drives our everyday existence. We cannot imagine, although we deeply long for, a life without the pervasive fear-induced adrenalin and cortisol that floods our bodies.

We may show, or hide, our gaps, or wounds, in different ways—and some people display them eagerly and openly in the hope of attracting sympathy, care and support from other people. Other wounded souls distract themselves from their own emotional bleeding by caring for other people, and having a sense of being needed by, and therefore of some worth to, another. Others withdraw into a back-room of their lives to avoid the need for interaction with people. A few retreat into the dark cellar of their lives, leaving only a socially acceptable persona behind which deals with their everyday lives but remains disconnected from their deeper feelings and needs. With empathy and deep sensitivity I name these folks the 'cellar-dwellers' as they choose, from feelings of intense fear and dread of exposure, to stay in the lonely darkness to protect their illusion of safety. That very choice only widens their gaps into deep crevasses, and keeps them further away from the very things that could heal their gaps. I have found both personally and professionally that academic degrees and professional qualifications do not fill gaps—although they can provide a smokescreen that tricks people into believing that no gaps exist. A great many damaged souls have been motivated to improve their sense of worth and validity by accruing impressive qualifications, but these are no substitute for having a heart that is capable of loving and being loved.....the very thing that our gaps can block. The majority of relationships can be described as dysfunctional, wherein damaged people—with their own significant gaps—find other damaged people to have an entanglement/relationship with, and perhaps have children together. They try, for a while at least, to conceal, or to anaesthetise, the experience of their gaps; and the cycle continues—due to ignorance and the lack of the opportunity to learn, change and grow as a human soul. Such opportunities are long overdue, but I sincerely hope that the modules of 'The Ripple Effect' Process will provide them, and thereby help people in a new and vital way.

It is no surprise that as a nation of inadequate parents we are also a nation of dog lovers. Bonding with a pet which shows you unconditional love and attention releases Oxytocin in your system which makes you feel good, because you are wanted and needed. We may not have had good emotional attachments with family members, but we can still attach to an animal as a substitute. (I did just that myself, until one day I returned from school to be told by my mother that she had taken my young dog Susie to the vets to be 'put-down'. I was heartbroken—although I didn't waste my time showing it and instead I stuffed it down with the rest of the pain and despair I felt. I kept different dogs for over 20 years after I left 'home'.)

In our celebrity obsessed culture we want to elevate the beautiful and talented to great heights so that we can revere, envy and emulate them. We can also find a place to belong within a group of like-minded followers linked to these celebrities. Then we become mean and we look for their shame, their shortcomings.....their gaps. Time after time the media and paparazzi vividly and cruelly show us the celebrity's gaps, and we are apparently 'shocked' to find that they are as flawed as we are after all. Singers, athletes, politicians, media personalities, models, and anyone else in the public eye, are walking a tightrope of shame when they become famous. We want to think of them as perfect and better than ourselves in some significant way; but we also want to hear about the ways in which they have disappointed us, and how their human failings have now been exposed to the hungry mob. We can use social media sites to share with our group/tribe/clan how disappointed and betrayed we feel. Focussing on someone else's deficits, faults, and mistakes helps us to feel temporarily elevated, and gives us the opportunity of avoiding focussing upon, or exposing, our own shameful gaps.

Our gaps can serve us well—once we have learned how to slowly soothe them and begin to fill them in with understanding, compassion and sensitive care for the mosaic of our lives. I have tried hard to fill in my own gaps, and also to help others to do the same. I have spent many years and many thousands of pounds attempting to carry out this service for myself and for my clients. I have been the most successful in recent years. Not from the four years of psychotherapy I had as part of my professional training (from which I learned that I am competitive, that I compare myself with others a lot of the time, and that I didn't freely show my emotions. I probably already knew that). What I did receive was the time to tell my story, month after month and year after year. To find my voice and to be heard—although the few times I noticed my therapist stifling a yawn did knock me back a little, and challenged my right to be there and to be heard! I later learnt a great deal from group work and particularly inner child work—which is the root of the wounding and the basis of real and longer-term healing. From a place of not even knowing what happiness actually was, let alone whether I felt that I deserved it, or how to find and sustain it; I have now reached a vantage point where I can have a life that isn't holding me down in a pit of fear and struggle, of conflict and competition, or of loneliness and enforced independence. I now have the richness of love in my life, real and unconditional friendships, simplicity, clarity, calmness and a bright future ahead. I have clear boundaries that exclude the fear-and-shame-driven people, who only want to use, abuse, and take all they can to meet their own needs, and who sadly still lack the capacity to love.

I have created 'The Ripple Effect' Process because I want to share what I have learnt with as many people as possible. I wish I'd had access to 'The Ripple Effect' Process myself 30 years ago! It would have saved me many years of anxiety, fear, sadness, several dysfunctional relationships and a fragile self-esteem. But if I'd been fortunate enough to have found 'The Ripple Effect' I wouldn't be who and where I am now....and offering you some of the insights from my own long and ongoing journey.

We cannot climb a ladder starting from the middle rung—even if we were flexible enough, our own body weight and gravity would see to that! Instead we must climb from the bottom rung upwards, one rung at a time. In the same way we need to stand firmly on each rung of the ladder of our own lives, which then gives us a sound footing from which to climb higher. These lower rungs represent the physical, emotional and cognitive/mental aspects of our lives. 'The Ripple Effect' Process has been designed to address these levels throughout the modules, which then frees people up to climb onto the higher rungs of their spirituality. To prematurely jump up to our spiritual level without first having the grounding of the earlier levels leaves us with more gaps. We might assume the identity of a spiritually enlightened soul but our earthly difficulties such as an unhealthy imbalanced body, erratic moods, hyper-emotionality, and irrational thinking processes will all bring us crashing down with at least a few bruises!

PROFESSIONAL GAPS

Continuing with the house analogy—where can we go to find the help we need to create a strong, stable, resilient and safe home out of the shell of the building we have brought with us from childhood?

We need professional and expert help, from an architect with the knowledge, intuition and foresight to take on the whole project and not to cut corners along the way. We need sound advice, new knowledge and awareness, and most importantly to be taught the skills we will need both to carry out the renovation, and to continue to maintain the home in the good condition it deserves. If we simply carry on living in a rickety old shed we will not be protected from the elements and will deny ourself the warming hearth and cosy home that the child within so desperately wants and needs.

Imagine you are to be the project manager of such a renovation. You may have sought and received recommendations about where to find the help you need for such a project, which will reassure you and bring you the hope and expectation that you will get all the support and advice that you will need along the way. Imagine too that you decide to go along to an Ideal Home Exhibition to look at the stands and to find out what each method of renovation and repair (therapy) has to offer you. As you walk in, you notice how bright, shiny and appealing everything looks: it offers an unspoken promise that your inner-home will one day look like this and evoke the same feelings of comfort, ease and security. There are an array of stands, behind each of which you see a particular therapist who beckons you to come and hear what they have for you. Any one of the many types of counselling or psychotherapy on offer cannot do all that you need, and despite many months, or even years, and the huge expense incurred, you will still be left with a shaky structure and, if you are lucky, a few flimsy plans about what needs doing—if only you knew how to carry them out!

THE PSYCHOANALYTIC STAND

This stand is bare and barren and gives away nothing of the person sitting behind the screen into which you are expected to speak, at length. You may have realised that this is the original form of psychotherapy from which many of the subsequent models derived, and that it has been established for a very long time. The expectation of you is that you attend at least twice a week, perhaps as often as five times a week. You may be invited to lie on a couch and the analyst will say very little to you at all, despite their sitting near to you in the same room. They will not form a two-way relationship with you, and you will have the silence in which to form your own personal insights and associations, and to vocalise them. There will, in time, be a 'third' presence in the room—that of your sub-conscious 'meta-communication' which envelops what you are saying, as it silently expresses to the analyst what you really, although unknowingly, mean. You will become aware that you have three distinct parts to you: namely your Ego—which defends itself in a wide variety of ways; your Id—which is your more instinctive, spontaneous and primitive self; and your Superego—which is the observer of yourself and which directs and guides your life, whether that be towards a life instinct or a death instinct. Your sexual energy and its expression or repression also feature largely in the diagnosis, by the analyst, of your difficulties—although this will not be shared with, or explained to, you. You continue to come back here for many years but you will not be guided towards the ways in which you might improve the fabric and structure of your abode.

The Psychodynamic stand

Again the therapist says very little, and certainly not about themselves, and they do not offer any opinions or make any suggestions to help you along in your quest to renovate your house. As with all therapies you may occasionally be asked leading, or open, questions to get you going and to help you to speak about the difficulties you have had in your childhood that have lead to the structural problems with your house. The therapist is again a blank screen upon which you are expected to project aspects of your own history—as if the therapist actually was a person from your past; or someone who, in the present moment, evokes your old historical responses to their present-time silence and non-engagement with you. You may speak at length about your history, and the therapist will become aware of how they are feeling in relation to you—this is called their counter-transference—which is either in response to your transference onto them of the characteristics or expectations of someone else who actually was present in your earlier life; or it may simply be aspects of their own personal history that have been activated by what you have been saying and the way in which you communicate with them. You will probably be expected to work with this therapist for a long time, but are unlikely to come away with any clearer idea about how to tackle the renovation project that is still waiting to be started.

The Cognitive stand

There are different branches, or subdivisions, in this therapeutic approach. You may be offered rational-emotive therapy which focusses, as the name suggests, upon your thoughts and the way in which they affect your feelings and emotions. You may instead be offered cognitive-behavioural therapy which will use as its focus your irrational thinking processes, and will then offer you ways to change these, and thereby change the ways in which you feel and behave. Whilst addressing an important aspect of your difficulties, this method will not include your past and the way in which it has shaped the cracks, rot and damp of your home. Instead it will give you plenty of helpful advice on how to cover over, and hide, the cracks and this may convince you, and others, that all is well—until the cracks and gaps reappear, perhaps somewhere else in the house because you won't have learnt how not to recreate more problems for yourself. You may rectify some faults only to have them replaced with new ones!

If the therapist were to offer you Transactional Analysis as a method of help then you would gain greater insight into how your problems arose, how they are sustained, and even some ways to change them. This is a comprehensive and relatively quick method of therapy with something tangible to take away with you. However, it won't address some significant aspects associated with the structural faults such as your feelings and how to regulate them, or how to change your negative thought processes which exacerbate your difficulties. Neither will it look at the bigger picture of your life and how your current problems relate to this; or how you might elevate yourself into a more mindful, balanced and rewarding way of life, with the tools to fix-up the house and deal with any ongoing and persistent problems.

THE PERSON-CENTRED STAND

Here you can expect to be repeatedly asked how you feel about something and everything! You may be here for months, and whilst you enjoy being listened to—and you may have even come to quite like the long silences—you won't come away with anything new. It is believed by the therapist that you hold the blue-print and architectural drawings that you need for the project ahead; and if they sit alongside you and ask how you feel about the cracks, draughts, wonky walls and gaps in the floorboard, that you will have a "Eureka!"—or "Ah-ha!"—moment and suddenly have all the answers you need. Whilst this approach was a welcome warming up of the previously cold and emotionally distant therapist of years gone by, it will become clear that you will not actually get what you have paid for, and you may well come to believe that this is in some way your fault. You can expect the therapist's positive regard for you, their stance of non-judgement—as far as this is humanly possible—and their congruence (which means that they will display on the outside what is going on for them on the inside). These are the core conditions of the training in this style of therapy. You will be asked open questions, and your responses will be reflected back to you, and may be summarised or paraphrased for you—just in case you were not clear about what you have said. It is a popular starting point for trainee therapists but you will no doubt need much more than this approach to enable you to have the confidence or skills for the hard task ahead.

THE GESTALT STAND

This stand may catch your eye with its bright colours and loose semi-bohemian influences. The therapist will be interested in your awareness of your body, feelings and sensations, as well as in your level of contact with your environment—and the ways in which you avoid deeper contact with other people in your field of experience.

They may offer you an empty chair or cushion to use in a two-way dialogue with yourself to uncover previously hidden aspects of yourself which may enlighten you as to how the structural faults have been set up, tolerated and endured by your 'Self'. You will probably find this method engaging and even fun. It traditionally did not concern itself with your history and developmental deficits but more recent trainings will now include these crucial aspects. Don't expect to come away with any specific help, advice or guidance; but you will be more aware of your situation and the way in which it impacts upon your psyche, and in turn upon the people around you.

The Trans-personal/Existential stand

You will definitely not get any advice or help here that you can use when you get home. The focus will be upon your higher self and your inner wisdom—which is still a valid and a vital part of who you are. It is perhaps a more relevant therapeutic approach to take when you have already put your house in order; otherwise your foundations will still be shaky whilst you are busy trying to fix solar panels to your roof. You will be invited to examine the deeper meaning and purpose of your life and soul journey, and of having this dilapidated house to fix up along the way. It is very important for you to have a workable plan and to follow it through with firm intention, determination and desire. You will therefore need more than this type of therapy if you are ever going to get started, or even to make a list of what needs doing and in what order, and by whom. Some you can do yourself—like clearing out the cluttered cupboards and disposing of the rubbish, but you still need professional guidance in your project that this method of therapy doesn't offer. It may be wise to come back here when the work is done if you'd like a higher, wider, deeper perspective on your life path and the meaning of your struggles.

If Psychosynthesis is on offer you will become acquainted with your sub-personalities. These are the offshoot personae set up by your younger mind in response to the pronounced emotional and psychological difficulties in your past. These are not multiple personalities—or dissociative identity disorder—but instead are like constant characters in the ongoing play of your life, who come out and onto centre stage when a particular cue or prompt arises. Each will have its own separate body language and even its own voice and script. Don't be scared by them. Many hands make light work and they may come in useful for the task ahead—as long as none of these sub-personalities inside you sabotages or otherwise derails the project for you. You may find that each one has been occupying their own room in your house for many years too. When the work is done you can invite what's left of them to the party!

THE CREATIVE/EXPRESSIVE STAND

At last...an opportunity for the projection and expression of your needs. But wait.... it may need to be in the form of your hidden inner creativity, desires and previously stifled voice! You may be encouraged to draw, paint, sculpt, make masks or models, or even engage in a mini drama vignette to expose and explore the hidden dynamics of your personality and character, and your relationship to your damaged house. Whilst a playful and entertaining distraction, this approach will not give you the tools to get started on your renovation project .... although you may enjoy the movements, music, shouting, chanting, colouring-in, cutting, painting and model-making.

THE COACHING STAND

Ah-ha....some much needed clarity, but alas much will also be missing from the overall picture of what you need. Whilst you will be encouraged to access your own common sense—by borrowing that of the coach—you will not have sufficient insight into the how and why of your unique problems to avoid them happening again. You will be given the opportunity to create your goals—with manageable strategies; but unless the deeper wounded part of you is on board with, and understands, the project, there is a good chance that you will scupper your own attempts. This may mean a need to have the coach alongside you for regular check-ins and top-ups, as the skills you may learn won't necessarily fit your own individual circumstances, but instead, may be the result of an off-the-peg, one-size-fits-all theoretical base to the coach's limited training. The coach is unlikely to have had their own therapy either and so there is the distinct possibility of their own cracks and deficits becoming present and affecting any work you might do together.

The Energy stand

Again it is likely that this therapist will not have had their own personal therapy and their training may well have been of very short duration and consist of the learning of a few simple techniques which they then pass on to their clients. Energy psychology and energy medicine do however also have their place in healing and can be an important adjunct to more meaningful and long-lasting insight, growth and change. You may be encouraged to tap certain points on your body and head—where these are will depend upon the therapist and the approach they are replicating with you. Visualisation, mindfulness and meditation, movement, music, breath-work, laughter and playfulness are all very significant aspects of an effective overall therapeutic approach, but are not in themselves enough for the task that lies ahead of you. Your foundations need sound underpinning which comes from something more solid than what you can expect from this therapist. You will be able to visualise and work towards your goals—which is vital to attaining them—but you will also need a good dollop of learning, understanding, and personal insight and skills along the way....so better move on to the next stand.

The Integrative stand

This therapist has realised that we are all complex and unique individuals who may have similar structural problems, but who will need different tools to deal with them, and different approaches to understanding the important 'how and why' of our problems too. This therapist will have been trained in a way that incorporates the research-based approaches shown to be the most effective and beneficial. They will be aware of your developmental needs and deficits, as well as helping you to access your emotions. Their training will probably still have its own gaps though—such as in the very significant cognitive aspects of who you are, your creativity, mindfulness, visualisation, meditation, and gaps in skills-training. Depending upon the individual therapist and how keen they have been to seek out additional trainings and experiences which they could then weave into their own way of working, you may get either a basic integrative therapist or an enhanced one—I hope for your sake it is the latter, who will be of much more help to you and provide you with much of what you want and need. You will certainly have enough to be able to make a noticeable improvement to your home.

So much for the Ideal Home analogy. I hope it, albeit somewhat tongue-in-cheek, gives you a brief idea of what to expect from each therapeutic approach—which all have their own particular benefits to offer you, as well as their own deficits, or gaps, too. I believe that what is most beneficial is an approach that combines the full presence of a therapist who has a genuine interest in, and an attunement to you, your history and your current needs and aspirations. Their knowledge and skills base should include human brain development, and up-to-date neuro-scientific research findings. I believe that the physical presence of the therapist is vital and so I am not enthusiastic about telephone counselling or even the more recent on-line video-link counselling. These methods are fine, up to a point; but a therapist cannot notice the tell-tale give away of the slight change in body language, especially in the eyes, of the client if they are not physically present with them. Neither can there be the spontaneous creative input which can be so revealing and rewarding. Your therapist should be looking at your past only with reference to the way in which it has shaped and influenced you, and the deeper hidden decisions you made back then, about the expectations you have of your life, and of other people. The therapist should help you to normalise and understand your current circumstances in the light and context of your past experiences. They should be comfortable with being open, authentic and even playful with you. They must of course work to ethical standards to ensure both your safety and that their professional boundaries remain intact. They should, ideally, be aware enough of themselves to be able to guide you, and your soul, on your journey during the brief time that they walk alongside you. They should be a confident, warm and clear communicator who feels at ease with using a diagram or illustration to help to explain something important to your understanding. They should not be bound by the simple replicating of the often modelled 'therapist pose' they will have absorbed during their training—which includes the slow nodding of their head—at a tilted angle—having a frown upon their sad face, and a circular wrist-wave as if trying to coax something out of you. They should be aware of current thinking and theories and not be tied to those of previous generations, and more importantly, not treat these as secrets held close by the 'select few'—but instead to share them with you as desired and as appropriate to your needs. This description of a good therapist has become an important criterion in my selection of counsellors and psychotherapists to become authorised licensees to present the twelve psycho-emotional-educational modules of 'The Ripple Effect' Process. I also believe that a small safe group experience is a very significant and enriching one. We all grew up in a group and we all behave differently in a group from the way we do in one-to-one encounters. I have therefore ensured that learning, sharing, and forming deeper connections from a small group, is an integral part of 'The Ripple Effect' Process too.

I will now share with you how I joined up the dots in my own life to reach the point at which I am now writing this book with the heartfelt intention of helping you to fill in your own gaps and to join up your own dots.

Joining Up The Dots

The dots to be joined up are those moments or events that later turn out to have been significant markers along the path we have taken that brought us to where we are now. We may not have seen them at the time they emerged, or realised their significance to us and the ways in which they would shape our future choices. If you look up into the clear night sky you will see an array of bright twinkling dots. Only when you can locate certain of these stars will you be able to join them up into a constellation which gives the individual stars a greater significance and meaning in relation to one another. Life gives us all such 'dots' along the way, and as we think back and make the connections between them, we can see how they have shaped different aspects of our lives and formed the constellation patterns of our relationships, friendships, work-life, and ultimately, how we have chosen to live our lives. My own relevant dots here are the ones which pointed me in the direction of creating 'The Ripple Effect' Process and of writing this book—a book that I have no idea if anyone will read, but which I hope will be of benefit to someone. So, I will now join up some of my own dots.

Having established that we all have our own gaps—which derive from our own unique histories—and also that there are significant gaps in the professional therapeutic services available, I set about creating something to fill in the professional gaps, which would in turn help people to fill in their personal gaps. The current therapeutic approaches were created by men (for example Freud, Jung, Assagioli, Beck, Ellis, Berne, Perls, Rogers, Bandler, Riech), and yet have been taught to a very large number of predominantly female trainees, who would in turn become counsellors and psychotherapists working with a predominantly female client base. It was time for a new approach to therapy, created by a woman, yet available to everyone.

My own childhood gaps ached to be filled. My weekend drinking and partying certainly didn't fill them, in fact it only made them worse. We people with painful gaps often use alcohol to 'become someone else'—to take us away from the grim reality of our own gap-filled existence, to hide our vulnerability from ourselves in the hope that it will not still be there the next day when we become sober again. Paradoxically, alcohol increased my vulnerability, and most of the bad things that have happened to me as an adult have happened whilst I was drunk or because my drink had been 'spiked' with a drug to render me semi-conscious. I have nearly died because of someone else's selfishness. Chaotic and unstable relationships certainly didn't fill my gaps either—but I didn't know how to have any other sort of relationships at that time. My work and status in the civil service provided the money that I spent in my futile efforts to fill in my ever widening gaps. I bought lots of 'stuff'—the buzz of making a purchase never seemed to fade back then. I had a huge wardrobe of clothes,—in fact a whole colour scheme for each week for 8 weeks as I recall—and I went on holidays, bought cars, and went to lots of parties. I'd started working there at the age of 16, on the lowest grade, and yet gradually rose up through internal promotions to an executive role. I was entrusted with lots of responsibility which I knew that I could cope with and, in line with my need to be seen to be competent and effective, I was just that. I had to develop additional personae to enable me to face the abusive and aggressive claimants with whom I had to have contact—usually in their own homes. This was often dangerous and I was threatened several times. My own history proved to be an asset to me in these encounters as I had developed a tough sub-personality—validated as such on the occasions when I have been referred to as a 'formidable opponent'. The familiar smell of a certain type of benefit-claimant's home would cling to my clothes, and stick in my throat; and after a day of such unaccompanied visits I would go home and have to soak in the bath to rid myself of the cloying odour. I was fortunate that, unlike some colleagues at the time, I didn't have to be fumigated to kill off an infection of fleas or lice. I found out about the levels at which some people survive. This was all they knew and they saw nothing wrong with it. My judgement of their circumstances would have seemed alien to them. Generally, these were not people who had any interest in self-development. Their sole interest was in getting their basic needs met and fighting hard to do so whatever it took. Here was a 'dot' for me to join up with those of my own upbringing: the realisation of the very different levels at which people live, and the different values, beliefs, perceptions, needs, and interest—or lack of it—in their own self-awareness or personal development that many people have. There was of course a different type of claimant too; those whose temporary circumstances led to their current need for help, and they were usually ashamed of their need for financial assistance. Little did I realise back then that life would turn the tables on me and that I would find myself on the other side of the counter when I became a benefit claimant as a single-parent family without financial support for my child. Life can be such a leveller!

I had to learn how to switch and adapt myself from being a front-line investigator of frauds and failures to acknowledge parenthood or to pay child support, to presenting cases on behalf of the department for whom I worked, at the local magistrates and county courts, and having to converse confidently with solicitors and, occasionally, barristers. A false-self is hard to maintain over any length of time and it becomes very draining—emotionally, psychologically and spiritually. I grew to hate my job. I was the proverbial square peg in a round hole—which was a familiar feeling for me. I'd had what I later realised was mild depression and a frightening panic attack, before I finally left that job, after having endured it for 12 years, in order to try to reclaim my own identity and life-path—whatever that was. I was determined to find out. I needed help but I had no idea where to look for it, so I carried on wearing the familiar mask which convinced people that I was having a good time. I wasn't mentally ill and in need of psychiatric help, and I hadn't heard of counselling back then in the mid 1980's, so I just plodded on with the next challenge or distraction from finding myself and what I really wanted and needed. Whenever any of my dreams nowadays include seeing myself back there working in that job I know it is a sign to me that I am stuck, stagnant and screaming silently to myself to change the direction of my life, and to live more in tune with who I really am. Here too, I now see was a dot.... my own need to change and find out about myself and who I was and who I could become.

Knowing that I wanted to do something which would help people in some way, I began a course in beauty and body therapy—which was ironic considering that I'd been called 'ugly duckling' in my family (I often consoled myself with the ending of the story—the emergence of the swan—and the phrase "just you wait and see!") My five car accidents, as well as numerous physical assaults had resulted in my having a crooked broken nose—which only increased the name calling .....sadly my own family were the worst culprits. Damaged people try to make other people feel worse than they do, even their own children. Isn't it strange too how the odd overheard comment can radically impact you? I remember once standing behind a man at a bar (surprise, surprise) who was saying to my boyfriend at that time (and my daughter's biological father-to-be), that if it wasn't for my nose I'd be attractive. That small observation felt like a branding iron hissing upon my bare skin, and I was engulfed in shame—for having the sort of family that could have let things happen to me that caused my nose to be the obstacle to my being seen as attractive. In the science subjects associated with my beauty therapy studies I was getting exam results in the 90% range and found that although this path and profession would have been easy for me, in many important ways it just wasn't a good 'fit' with me. I didn't have the easy dazzling smile and convincing mask of the perfectly groomed and made-up beauty therapist. Neither did I relish the prospect of performing further pedicures on people who didn't show me the basic courtesy of at least having clean and fungus-free feet; or of doing another bikini-line and arm-pit hair-removal wax on the 'unwashed'. I needed to rethink. It was the wrong sort of therapy for me, but it did open my eyes to other forms of therapy namely aromatherapy, reflexology, diet and nutrition, and shiatsu massage which I then went on to study too. The dot here was the realisation that I wanted to offer some form of therapeutic service that was of real benefit to people.

During this beauty therapy training course I had become pregnant. This was certainly not planned, and I would not have thought it physically possible to happen when it did during my menstrual cycle. I had earlier been told by my doctor that it was unlikely that I would be able to carry a baby to full-term, due to the damage caused by one of the sexual assaults I had experienced. I'd had two negative pregnancy tests and dismissed the changes in my body as due to hormone imbalances caused by stress..... but my daughter was clearly determined to be born to me. Later, when I'd had a positive pregnancy test I was by then a few months pregnant, and despite the shock of this news I decided then and there that I had to radically change my lifestyle—to one better suited to the embryo slowly growing inside me—whether or not it resulted in the birth of a living child. I didn't even buy any equipment until I was about 30 weeks pregnant in case I didn't need it. On one of my examinations I was told that my baby appeared to have a deep crevice across her head but not to worry as there would be help available for such a disabled child......it turned out that she was in the breech position, and that wasn't her head that they'd been feeling! The many sleepless nights of worrying about my future with a disabled child proved to have been needless when she was born healthy and just two weeks prematurely. I've never had much faith in the conventional medical profession. When I'd found out that I was in fact, by some miracle, pregnant my boyfriend, although a teacher who professed to love me, decided that he "didn't want the responsibility" of a child and pushed an envelope through my door which contained the money for me to have an abortion. I deposited the money into a bank account for my daughter. I was used to having to deal with big challenges and this was just the latest one to hit me. With hindsight I would have realised just how big and life-changing becoming a parent, let alone a single-parent with no support at all, would be. Having my daughter was the catalyst for a huge change in my life and a good and timely reason for me to evaluate my lifestyle and what I wanted in the future for myself and my daughter.

There were two highly significant dots here for me. The first was my need to find out why someone would or could behave as he had done. His abandonment of us, without further contact or any ongoing financial help shocked me to my core. I just didn't understand how he could behave like that—it seemed so out of character. I obviously hadn't known the real him at all! I actually now have a lot to thank him for—but I haven't done so, and probably never will. I hear that he didn't get married or have any more children. I guess he really needed to avoid any responsibilities after all. He is a stranger to us, but one whom I probably understand more than he understands himself, thanks to the path I took and his unintentional involvement in that path.

The second dot was my new-found hunger to learn about myself and how I could actually make the changes in myself that I wanted and needed in order for me to become a good parent and to give my child much better parenting than I had experienced myself.

One day, when my baby daughter was a few months old, I left college early and went to collect her from a neighbouring childminder's house. It broke my heart to see my little baby girl alone in a room, motionless and looking sad and withdrawn in her bouncy cradle whilst the other children were in the next room laughing and watching television. I immediately gave up the college course. I think I knew back then that I probably wouldn't use the qualifications that I missed out on receiving anyway. That course, or the two-thirds of it that I completed were only a stepping stone for me.

I soon felt that my brain was becoming lazy through lack of exercise. There is only so much story reading and children's TV that an adult mind can take! I found out about local classes run by the Workers Education Association, and that literally changed the course of my life. There was a well-run creche there and I attended highly subsidised classes four mornings a week for an hour and a half a day. My classes were in a wide and eclectic range of subjects, but most importantly in biology and genetics (and I had a great tutor, called Brian, who laughed like a braying donkey but was otherwise truly inspirational); and a four-year course in child and personality development (which was tutored by a diminutive, but in many ways statuesque, man called Ed who will never know how great his impact was upon me).

The dots to be joined up here were the realisation of how transforming both a small group dynamic and an interesting topic could be; as well as the ability to make friends and keep in touch with other group members—something that I later found to be lacking in psychotherapy groups due to the boundaries imposed upon members. I also signed up for my first Introduction to Counselling in 1988 which started me on a long and circuitous, but nevertheless engrossing and richly rewarding journey.

As the counselling course progressed I realised that what was on offer in the training programme fell very far short of what people like myself, with gaps, would really need; but it was a good enough starting point. It was a person-centred course and with it I combined additional studies in Gestalt and Transactional Analysis methods. I became a voracious reader and spent all I could afford to spend on buying books that I could own, and so be free to annotate them as I wished. In time, the amount of my learning surpassed the level needed for working with clients in a private practice—who were, after all, predominantly people who were able to function well enough to work and who could afford to pay for private counselling services.

In 1998 I embarked upon a four-year Masters Degree in Integrative Psychotherapy; and here too I felt frustrated because, as I saw it, so much time was wasted on extraneous subjects and not on fundamental core topics like neuro-scientific research findings about the working of the brain. Here was more irony….a psychotherapy training course that spent so little time on the development and workings of the brain—the very organ which is clearly integral to the profession! The gaps in both the training material and the overall training process were obvious to me, and I realised that I would need to spend much more of my own time and money in filling these professional gaps myself, in order for me to provide a better service for my clients. This was a university validated four year course and yet still there were still significant gaps in it. Other shorter and more superficial training courses cannot help but leave 'qualified' therapists with even larger gaps in their levels of knowledge and skills.

There is a lot of shaming, envy and competition between members of the various therapy-training groups and counsellor-supervision groups that I've experienced, both personally, and from what I've heard from colleagues' and peers' experiences. I have also encountered needy and greedy egos in some of the therapists I've met. Much to my surprise and disappointment at the time, I became aware that some of them also had alcohol and marijuana dependency problems too! It is commonly acknowledged that the profession attracts wounded souls looking for their own healing, and that training to become a psychotherapist happens by default for many people after they have had their own long-term psychotherapy as a client. This then combines with their need to feel of worth and value by being of service to others. I think it vital that all therapy training includes long-term therapy for the trainees. Not of the usual meandering or superficial types of therapy, but of a mixture of methods, styles and theoretical backgrounds. The conventional adherence to the one method and theory of a particular guru, (and later adopted by the associated training institute), restricts the perspective and skills of the newly emerging therapist. The dot here was my realisation of the different levels of personal development of qualified counsellors and psychotherapists—which dispelled my previously positive projection and assumption that all therapists would be somehow 'sorted', healed and gap-free. I would need to choose wisely the therapists with whom I would associate myself professionally.

During the time I was training to be a psychotherapist I was also fostering 'hard to place' teenage girls—which was demanding and rewarding in equal measure. I had also trained to be a kinesiologist—a very broad form of complementary therapy which includes health, diet and nutrition, and rectifying the many physical imbalances within the body—and this further informed my private practice. I had realised that no amount of talking therapy would help someone whose anxiety, depression or mood swings were caused by physical imbalances—such as those associated with their thyroid functioning, their blood-sugar levels, hormones, candida, parasites, food sensitivities and much more. I combined what I had learned about the body, health and nutrition, energy medicine and energy psychology, with my counselling and psychotherapy knowledge. There were still some gaps and these poked me and irritated me into finding out even more. In 2004 I put together the material for two groups, one called 'Understanding Yourself' and another called 'Understanding Relationships'—under the umbrella title of 'Psyche-Bytes'—and I set about advertising and running these. I did not realise at the time that this would become the starting point for the comprehensive programme of current workshops and ongoing groups of 'The Ripple Effect' Process. Another dot.

I had, by 2006, built up a busy practice in the Midlands; and yet I was restless. My supervisor at that time likened me to Sisyphus. Not knowing who this was, and as usual being too ashamed to admit this deficit in my education and knowledge, I looked it up and found that this particular mythical character was renowned for pushing a big boulder up a hill only to let it roll down the other side, when he would then have to resume the struggle of pushing it up the hill again. The analogy fitted well. I was successful, but nevertheless I was in need of another hill and another, and bigger, boulder. I didn't necessarily want to be like Sisyphus, but that was all I knew and the only alternative seemed to be like existing on a featureless plateau—and that image bored, and also frightened, me. I could die alone on that plateau, never having achieved anything of value or merit. I had to press on and keep myself alive with new challenges. I decided to move abroad for my next challenge.

After a few visits and some research I chose Portugal as the country to move to. I'd made a couple of friendly contacts and was intent upon a new experience as a therapist to the 'ex-pat' community in the Algarve region, where they mostly reside. A cancer scare and subsequent treatment put paid to that plan, as did my daughter having a car accident. I could not be as far away from her as Portugal was in case she needed me, even though she was 20 years old. My compromise was to stay in the UK but to live near the sea in a relatively warm and sunny area—which narrowed it down to the south coast of England. After a few fact-finding trips I decided upon a place to live. The sea was in front of me and the hills of the South Downs were behind me. I felt that I could at last take a deep breath some 200 miles away from the stifling and landlocked Midlands area that I had lived in all my life.

My house in the Midlands didn't sell and after a year I re-mortgaged it—in the days when it was easy and common to do so—and I used the equity as a deposit on my seaside home-to-be. In the meantime I spent seven months in a cold, damp flat where I was frequently ill, but happy to be able to walk to the sea and sit alone in coffee shops watching people, and the tides, come and go. I didn't know anyone there but that felt fresh, new and exciting. I built up a small practice thanks to my website's prominence; and I set about organising my thoughts and my professional knowledge into what would later become 'The Ripple Effect' Process. I sorted through, and organised, the masses of notes, articles, essays, book references, handouts and much more that I had accumulated over the years. I had always felt deep down that I would one day need all of these and that I should keep them to hand. I then started to make hand-written drafts for several workshops and ongoing groups, but they were all still in a rough and basic form.

When I moved into my new-to-me, but old, Victorian house in the winter of 2007 I was distracted by the renovation work needed (another project!) and the problematic builders—which then resulted in the stress of a county court case. Eventually I found the right man for the job and the work progressed well, and so my stress levels reduced—although not entirely. I was having major problems with tenants and lodgers at my former home and had to travel the five hours each way most weekends to sort things out as best I could. I was profoundly disappointed to find out just how lacking in integrity some people could be. Their characters and personalities negatively impacted upon me—that was a ripple effect I could have done without! To compound my sense of disappointment in people I also had a relationship that would prove, over the next three years, to be very emotionally draining and exasperating.....but I have to say, another rich learning experience. We are here to learn, to experience and to thrive against the odds. Even the most difficult people and challenges are gifts to us. We may not appreciate that at the time, but later on we may see them as having been significant dots in our own constellations.

I also began to consider my next professional step. I was an established psychotherapist. I supervised the work of a few other counsellors, psychotherapists, and workers in community and local government projects.....and I was feeling stale. Having, mainly through my own efforts, accumulated masses of information, theories, skills and experience I felt somewhat frustrated that I was working predominantly with individuals and couples. I wanted to spread myself, and my message, further. I thought about embarking upon a PhD training but this left me feeling cold. I'd been resistant to the hoop-jumping needed to complete my Masters Degree, having felt irritated that I was being moulded into a researcher and writer of academically-based material, instead of being guided into becoming a fully competent psychotherapist. I also deeply wanted to create something that made a real difference to people's lives—and not just another lengthy thesis that would sit gathering dust in a cupboard somewhere. A major breakthrough for me was discovering the work of the neuroscientist and psychiatrist Dr Daniel Amen—at last the missing piece that gave the jigsaw of my work and studies a centrepiece! I read his books and integrated what I learnt into my own work. This was a major dot for me!

Over the years colleagues, peers, tutors and my own supervisors of my clinical practice had all commented upon my broad skills-base, my relentless quest for knowledge, and my determination to keep enhancing my skills, and to increase the tool-kit of what I had to offer both to my clients and to my supervisees alike. I took in this positive feedback and it bolstered my professional esteem, which in turn challenged my long-held negative self-belief system—something that four years of conventional therapy hadn't been able to change for me. I still believed myself to be a fraud on the cusp of being exposed and falling into the deep abyss of the shame that this would bring. However I really wanted to share out—in a positive ripple effect—all that I had learned over the years. I wanted both to educate people emotionally and psychologically, and to de-mystify therapy by sharing some important theoretical and experiential knowledge and skills with many more people.

Thanks to the annoyingly on-and-off nature of the relationship I was trying much too hard to stabilise and develop—and I'd previously promised myself not to take on any more fix-up-projects!—I spent a lot of time alone. Time that I'd expected to be spending doing 'couple stuff'—but he had what I later realised were profound difficulties with forming attachments and sustaining relationships. Difficult as this was to be on the receiving end of, it did free up my time to carry out additional research into the nature and origins of his complex problems—which I then also integrated into my work—as well as ensuring that I had the free time to carry on with my slowly emerging project of 'The Ripple Effect' Process. On reflection I can now see that the many dysfunctional relationships I have had over the last 35 years have actually been a catalyst to my finding out more about the troublesome behaviours that I encountered in each of these men. I have also had the time to understand my own part in each dynamic drama we played out together. Reluctantly I had to accept that I was on an ongoing 'rescue and repair' mission which was always doomed to fail because I was not able to be fully objective; and most importantly because I was neither their therapist nor their mother!

I had become so tired of being drawn into a man's life-drama and finding myself playing out a role assigned to me—either in order to help him to re-write his script, or just for him to repeat and reinforce it. It is one thing to know the theories about relationships but quite another to actually be a living part of one; particularly when someone has large gaps which they are too afraid to look at, let alone to try and fill. Or they deny that there is a problem, and they refuse to take any responsibility for repairing or improving the relationship. When the going gets tough it can be much easier for people with big gaps just to keep moving on to a new relationship, and the initial excitement and distraction that this brings. There's always another charismatic partner out there and another drama to be re-enacted—assuming that they are not too exhausted or despondent to bother looking again. I took time-out from relationships and spent it instead on my relationship with myself and on firming up 'The Ripple Effect' Process. Being alone brings me calmness, clarity and strength of purpose. I know that I can be all too easily distracted from this by someone else's needs, wants and preferences. I feel that I will soon be ready for the exploration of a new relationship—but not just yet. That will require me to search for the proverbial needle in a haystack when looking for a compatible partner. As we become more self-aware and live more from our heart and spirit, we need to attract similar people into our lives, and there are far fewer of these evolving souls around. I need to find someone who can enhance and enrich my life and who matches my energy and passion—and vice versa of course! It has become too difficult, and now even unthinkable, to just settle for Mr 60% and I am reminded that 'Like Attracts Like' in this universe! However, I have more work to do first—to promote 'The Ripple Effect' Process and for it to become well-known and of good use to the public. I also aim to make 'Quantum Psyche Process' well-known too. This is another valuable method of psychotherapeutic help that I have created, which focusses upon changing the sub-conscious belief system; but more of that in my next book!

Nowadays I live my life in a much simpler and lighter way. I check-in with myself regularly each day to see how I'm doing and what I want and need, and I try as best I can in the circumstances to get that, whether it be a need for solitude and calmness, simple food, to be in a natural environment, and to see things with my childlike-eyes of simplicity and straightforwardness. I no longer need piles of 'stuff' around me. Stuff drains my energy—it needs cleaning and polishing, repairing and maintaining, it costs me more than it gives me. I want assets not liabilities in all areas of my life. Having fewer responsibilities has freed me up to make the choices that better suit me. Less fear about my life releases me from the grip of stagnation.

It's strange, but often I have felt as if I'm just going through the physical motions of carrying out the steps that have already been ordained by a higher and wiser part of me. This has also happened with two subsequent projects—namely 'Higher Resonant Frequency' in 2010, and 'Quantum Psyche Process' in 2011, which I have created and set up websites for. It is as if I become a willing assistant in a process much bigger than the one I think I am involved in. Ideas would come to me at all hours—particularly when I was trying to get to sleep at night, and when I woke first thing in the morning. Sometimes in the middle of the night—and I would have to scribble down odd words and ideas to look at with fresh eyes a few hours later in the daylight and incorporate them into the overall process that I was piecing together.

I thought of an acronym that fits the process I went through in creating the psycho-emotional-educational modules of 'The Ripple Effect'—I CAN SEE IT!

I—Information

C—Collation

A—Assimilation

N—Negation—of extraneous and irrelevant information

S—Systematisation

E—Elucidation

E—Education

I—Integration

T—Transformation

I know ..... I'm a bit of a geek, but I like my geeky persona too, it contrasts with and complements my others so well!

I spent a great many hours huddled over my laptop and by mid 2009 I had ten modules—the last two of the final twelve emerged a few months later in Spring 2010—as well as the paperwork and contract agreement that made up the structure of the business that I wanted to build. I am passionate about helping people to understand and use relevant knowledge, skills and experiences that can change their lives for the better. I really wanted to create something that could do this, as well as making it inexpensive and therefore available to a wider range of people who were interested in their own personal and spiritual development.

The next step was to establish if there was a 'market' for my ideas and new project. Perhaps I had been deluding myself as to its appeal and, risky as it felt, I needed to find out—and to do the research and ask the right questions of the right people. I had reluctantly been trained in research methods as part of my psychotherapy training—something I had felt at the time to be an annoying waste of my time; but here I had a use for it beyond the academic expectations of my training course. I was delighted to get positive feedback from my research about the overall concept, the perceived gap in the market and the specific format of 'The Ripple Effect' Process. Some of the feedback I received included the desire for more psychologically-inclined information without the need to undertake an A level or degree in psychology, or a counselling training course in order to get it.

I then 'went back to the drawing board' several times, fine-tuning, amending and refining several aspects of the programme until I felt satisfied with it, and confident about how helpful it would be both to the public, and to those counsellors who wanted to increase the breadth of their own knowledge and learn additional skills with which to expand the services they had to offer to the public. I have also been very fortunate to find someone with patience, humour and integrity who lives close by, and who has helped me to fill in some my own gaps when it comes to technology! It feels good to be able to rely upon Darren Hurley for the things that I cannot do myself, and for which I have neither the time nor the inclination.

After having, up until then, presented much of the material myself, and having received some valuable testimonials; I had to again revise and expand the modules to include instructions that enabled someone else—a licensee—to present the workshops and groups themselves. I also had to find out about, and adhere to, copyright laws relating to the material. I have in turn become wise to the need for this to protect my own work as best I can from the possibility of intellectual property theft by people who don't have the knowledge or ability to create their own project of this type and standard. Finally having the modules printed felt so rewarding and exciting. It made the years of hard work feel really worthwhile. The hardest part was yet to come however with the challenges of recruiting licensees to present the modules on behalf of my new company; as well as 'marketing' the project to the public...... and thereby spreading the word, and the ripple, wider.

In 2010 I took advantage of free business advice offered from the government via local business links—which was actually of little help and if anything it set me back and caused me to waste money I didn't have. The marketing advice and income forecasts were way off line. Naively, expecting a torrent of interest from existing counsellors in my new and wonderful project, I had turned down work with new clients and consequently my income shrivelled. I was convinced that as soon as other therapists realised what a much needed and valuable project this was—and that it could really enhance their own private practice and income—they would be bashing down my door to get to it. Wrong! I did get a lot of response to my ads but not the genuine and positive response I was expecting and hoping for. I had made mistakes by following the business advice. I had ignored my gut instincts in favour of projecting 'expertise' onto business advisers whom I thought were experts. I had overlooked the fact that the counsellors and psychotherapists that I was looking for would be primarily motivated from the heart, and by the desire to help others, and not by the mildly aggressive marketing I had been guided to put out—which focussed instead upon how much money could be earned from the project.

I felt bruised and ashamed of my silly, yet fundamental, mistakes. I needed to follow my own heart and put myself in the place of someone looking anew at the recruitment advertisement in the professional journals in which they appeared. I had to ask myself, "if it were me reading this what would appeal to me?" and later, in revising the costings, "If it were me applying to become a licensee, what cost would I consider to be fair and reasonable?" I then scaled down the size and costs of the recruitment advertising—having wasted a few thousand pounds already. I rewrote the ads with a softer and more heartfelt message—and I attracted a different response. Of course, many were from counsellors who were just curious about the new project and had no genuine interest in becoming a licensee. Some said that they were already too busy, others, to my shock and dismay, were hostile and rude—belittling my efforts and accusing me of trying to take away their clients and livelihood. They could not have been more wrong! Offering people the opportunity to access brief, effective and affordable help would have a positive knock-on effect to the profession, but they just couldn't see this. Other responses were from counsellors who were simply unsuitable—which fortunately caused me to really focus upon the personal and professional qualities that I wanted to find in a prospective licensee. Despite my own earlier experiences I had still been projecting only positive qualities onto my fellow professional counsellors and psychotherapists. To my great dismay I have since discovered that there are many types of people with similar qualifications in psychological therapies, but yet who have very different characters, and who still have their own largely unfilled gaps—despite having had their own personal therapy as part of their training requirements! Had I experienced some of their strange behaviours from my own clients, it would have provided rich ground for further exploration. I know only too well that a professional 'education' offers no guarantee of a stable character or an authentic and well-rounded personality. Gaps can be covered over by academic certificates, diplomas and degrees, fame, wealth and social status; but they will still show up when the professional or social mask slips. It always slips.

Since I qualified as a counsellor in 1994, and as a psychotherapist in 2002, there has been a huge rise in the number of training courses being set up. Thus has in turn lead to a massive increase in the number of counsellors and therapists churned out each year who are then chasing the same number of clients. The government initiative of Improved Access to Psychological Therapies also had a negative impact upon the livelihoods of many counsellors who were now struggling to make a living. I knew that the counsellors and psychotherapists that I chose to become licensees would have something different and unique to offer their clients, and thereby help the licensee to stand out from the ever expanding crowd of therapists who fill the pages of the steadily increasing number of on-line directories for counsellors.

I have also had to deal with challenges to the boundaries of the project and consequently I have had to add clauses in the contract to cover what I had previously considered to be matters of basic integrity—but it soon became clear that where money and business are concerned, integrity can lapse and greed and personal gain can then push their way in. In refining the project, the financial aspects, and its boundaries around how it can be presented to the public, I have become much clearer and happier with the end result. It has always been my way to take the long and circuitous route with all of the pitfalls and diversions along the way. There is no end to my journey, but I know that I, like everyone else, need to ensure that I have a reliable compass or guide along the way. Travelling alone has its risks as well as its delights.

I am now building up a team of licensees across the U.K. I have advertised the project in leading women's magazines and have had 38 of my own articles published on-line. The exposure of my views and professional knowledge was another big challenge to me, as was linking up to the social media sites that I have used to help make the public aware that 'The Ripple Effect' Process exists. The website has always had a good supply of traffic, and to my great surprise, from every continent in the world! I know that anything new takes as long as it takes to become known and integrated. This is now happening, and I am so appreciative that the project is finding its place and becoming more widely known. I have spent the last few months focussing on advertising and marketing—something I would have abhorred in the past—but that was more about not wanting to put myself forward because this brings with it the potential for ridicule and attack. Well, that comes anyway so you might as well step out of the shadows and learn to take it. Initially, I didn't mention anything about myself on the website or in the information package I sent out to prospective licensees. This omission created doubts about the integrity of the project and, interestingly, projection onto it of falsehood—or rather that it was too good to be true, or some sort of con, scam or pyramid selling; it is none of these. I took a few deep breaths, chatted with my inner voice of doubt, and then included information about myself and about the creation of the project with prospective licensees. I even included my photograph on the website. The feedback from the licensees that I have subsequently interviewed has been positive. They felt that the project had my expertise and integrity attached to it and they also said that they liked there being a 'figure-head' too. I've never seen myself as a figure-head and I can only hope that I do the title justice.

The next step, both for myself and for the project is the writing of this book. Again I was fortunate, or perhaps guided, when I found the quality and clarity of professional advice and guidance that I was looking for, from attendance at a writer's workshop set up by the publishers Hay House, in London in early March 2012. I have been familiar with the work of the company's founder Louise Hay—a rare woman in a man's world 25 years ago when she self-published her first book about self-healing; and I liked the ethical stance and the subject matter of the books they publish. I had found another good fit. On the rare occasions this happens it just feels so right at the core. It is as it should be.

Over the last 25 years I have, perhaps like you, read a great many self-help and personal/spiritual development books. Some of these books have truly earned their place and have offered to hungry souls, a light along a short section of a darkened path of life. Many books say the same thing—but in a slightly different way. Many take one simple truth or piece of wisdom and spin it out into a whole book which is then so thin and repetitive that it leaves me wishing they had just condensed it into its rightful form of a chapter at most. There are also some very good books in this genre which include the accumulation of, and the results of research into, a wealth of other people's ideas, and they do not make any pretence to originality. They condense and present the work of others into a pleasant and informative reading experience. Others are so esoteric and intellectually challenging that they can be repellent and hard to assimilate in any meaningful way. We cannot live in a world of words alone. We become confused by, and paradoxically alienated from, the very guru figures whose intention it is to unite us back into the one-ness of our being. Copious words, meandering ideas and theories can all become just a screen—which deflects you from your own inner source of wisdom—onto which you are expected to project your own signal of agreement, loyalty and compliance to someone else's ideas about you. We cannot easily and effectively find our way through the forest of 'blah-blah-blah' found in this deluge of words, hype and 'motivational' speaking. We all need to learn, to understand, and to be able to relate this new understanding to our own history; to explore our experiences; to develop new skills that bring us lasting and desired changes; and then to integrate these so that we can enhance who we are, and enjoy a higher resonant frequency and elevated vantage point in our lives.

An analogy using The Chakra System may be useful here before I move on—incidentally, I intentionally raise the energy of my chakras every day and so this analogy personally fits for me. Every morning, before having my shower, I sweep up my body with the palms of my hands as I envisage and energise:

> The base of my spine—the area associated with my physical and sexual energy, and I envisage a deep red ruby gemstone here.
>
> My lower belly—associated with my emotional energy; and a rich orange amber gemstone.

My solar plexus—expressing my mental and cognitive energy, my will-power and ego, and a yellow gemstone Citrine.

My heart—my connection with love, harmony and balance, and my connection to the rest of the Universe, it is accompanied by an emerald gemstone

My throat—being my energy of creativity and self-expression, and the vivid gemstone turquoise.

My pineal gland/central forehead—being representative of my insight and clarity ; and the deep blue of a sapphire.

The crown of my head—being the energy of Universal wisdom, and the Universal language of love. I also focus here upon my energy of courage, tenacity, determination and resilience; and ultimately of deep gratitude for all that is and will be. This is where I see my connection to the Matrix, which connects us all with the energy of consciousness. The brilliant diamond symbolises this area for me.

So, back to the plethora of books on the market in this genre. They all focus upon at least one of these chakra energies, and they offer you a way of polishing up one, or perhaps two, of the associated gemstones. This may be a book about the physical and sexual body; or the emotions and how to acknowledge and/or change them; or the mental and cognitive functions, and again, how to become more aware of them and to change them; or the heartfelt-self and our connection to ourselves, past and present, as well as our connection to others and to the universal energy in which we all bathe; or about our creative talents and ways to express them; or our intuition and spiritual awareness; and finally our one-ness with every subatomic particle in the universe/multiverse. These are also dots to be joined up! Like a string of beautiful shining jewels. We are all of these jewels and yet much more—that special something that we cannot clearly, concisely or convincingly describe in this three-dimensional world we all currently inhabit.

To return to my earlier, and more 'grounded', analogy in part one—life is like a ladder and we need to stand and balance ourselves on each rung before we can climb higher. We need to have understood, explored and perhaps changed aspects of our physical, emotional and cognitive/mental lives before we can benefit from the well-intentioned, but often misdirected, advice and guidance from the spiritual coaches and gurus who may have no idea about the gaps into which the rest of us have been falling for years. We need a comprehensive and integrated approach to well-being and not just a few jigsaw pieces which each focus upon just one or two aspects of our lives without showing us what the finished picture can look like.

I am told that the media don't take new ideas seriously unless there is a book to accompany them. I thought that my book would be so concise as to be more like a pamphlet—but whatever its size, the most important aspect for me was that it didn't contain chapters of fluff and waffle. I feel irritated reading fluff and waffle. Maybe there is some irony in that as you read this. I hope not. My humble aim is to write a book about the programme of Psycho-Emotional-Education (or PEE) that I have created, called 'The Ripple Effect' Process which encompasses many of these chakra energy levels, and ladder rungs, within its twelve modules. From the body and its physical experience, to the emotional, cognitive, and also the heartfelt connection to what is, to a greater creative form of self-expression, to enhanced knowing, insight and clarity; and a higher resonance and expression of who we are truly meant to be.

We owe it to ourselves to explore new places within ourselves, whilst we live out our lives for the briefest of moments in a linear time that doesn't even really exist. We must live in the day to day trivia of our earthly lives with our feet on the illusion of solid ground, to ensure that we can then safely explore our higher levels without floating off into some pseudo-spiritual mirage where we can get lost in someone else's truth about who we really are. We can learn how to enhance, and therefore to live better within, the temporary home of the spirit until such time as we return to our true home.

I wish for 'The Ripple Effect' Process to spread out its power for change across the country; and perhaps one day, across the wider waters and into other continents. As we individually change and grow we cannot help but affect the lives of others who also then change and grow too—and so the ripple expands ever outwards touching the lives, hearts and souls of those it meets.

Filling In The Gaps

$\mathcal{M}$any brave and often desperate people bring their gaps into the psychotherapist's office hoping for help. It takes courage to face our psychological and emotional problems and we may fear taking what feels like a huge risk. Many people therefore avoid such a risk and never undertake any form of therapy, because they fear that it will mean being unmasked and left deeply vulnerable, and not knowing how to live out their lives without their familiar game-playing, roles and script. Only when their unstable moods and patterns of unwanted behaviours start to cause them major problems in their daily lives, or threaten their relationships, or the way in which they raise their own children, do they finally accept that they need help. They then have to try and find something and someone suitable to help them—which can be problematic and off-putting in itself as there are a myriad of therapy options out there all offering to be the answer. The therapy directories are full of potential therapists, but how do you know who will be right for you? It is a big expense in terms of both your time and money and yet a valuable investment in your future well-being if you make the right choice. Too often I have heard from a new client that they had previously been seeing a counsellor or psychotherapist for several weeks or months—or even years—and yet they still had the problems that they had initially sought help for!

The gaps that clients bring are often expressed externally as problems with their sense of worth and value; their sense of their own identity; problems in attracting or maintaining relationships—and even knowing what a good relationship looks like if they hadn't seen this when growing up; and of course the all-too-common problems of anxiety and depression in their may forms; and their difficulties with anger—either an inability to authentically and appropriately show it, or a tendency to squash it down and wear a happy compliant 'mask' to suit others' needs and expectations instead. Ultimately we all want to feel happier, more at ease within ourselves, to feel confident that we can cope with the inevitable challenges that we must meet. We want to be free from chronic upset and worry, and we want to live a full and rewarding life. Our gaps get in the way of all of these ambitions.

No matter what the 'presenting issue' is in therapy—whether it be self-harming, disordered eating, dependencies and addictions, mood swings, relationship and/or sexual difficulties, prolonged grief, anxiety disorders etc.—I see these as an expression of the deeper emotional and psychological wound that needs clearing out and cleaning up. We must then also learn not to pull off the scab prematurely, and instead to allow the wound to fully heal, and to learn how not to be wounded in that same way again.

Talking, in itself, does not fill in your gaps. Learning and understanding about your gaps, and hearing about other people's struggles and triumphs with similar gaps can normalise your own struggle and also encourage you to learn how to write new, affirming and positive chapters in the book about the rest of your life. We all need knowledge but we also need use-able skills that we can put into practice when required, and which then assist us in regulating our moods and in communicating more positively both to ourselves in our inner dialogues, and with other people. For these reasons I created 'The Ripple Effect' Process in its form of 12 'modules', each of which addresses a particular issue that is very relevant to our gaps, and each of which offer an understanding of them, and the opportunity to learn how to fill and heal them. I like clarity and I wanted the titles of the modules to reflect this, and so they all begin with either 'How

To....' or 'Understanding.....' I will now speak a little about each of the topics covered in the modules and how they individually impact upon us; as well offering suggestions to help you with each of these. I also mention what you could expect should you decide to attend that particular module of 'The Ripple Effect' Process yourself, although that is not the sole aim of this book.

Anyone can attend as many modules as they wish to—there is no obligation involved. The more you attend the more you learn and the greater the potential for change. Attending all twelve modules, at only £12.50 an hour (2012) would be cheaper than six months of counselling or psychotherapy—the main difference being that you would learn a huge amount and acquire the valuable skills necessary to enable you to make real changes in your life. A life with fewer gaps is a better life!

I recently spoke to a lady who told me that she had spent nearly £2,000 on a quick-fix weight-loss programme which involved her taking liquid meal-replacements for 6 months. I asked her why she had become so over-weight, and after a moment of reflection she quietly said "because I was so unhappy." This confirmed, even further, the need and relevance of 'The Ripple Effect' Process....to deal with many of the underlying problems that present themselves in so many ways in our lives, and yet for which we all want a 'quick-fix'.

These modules are designed to be of benefit to the general public. As I have said previously, I am particularly keen to attract mothers and mothers-to-be onto the modules because as they learn to understand themselves, regulate their emotional state and have a better relationship with themselves; then they will be more attentive and competent as parents, better able to raise the next generation with love, care understanding, and clear boundaries.....and so the ripple expands further.

UNDERSTANDING ANXIETY

I start here because anxiety is the most common expression of our gaps and it comes in several debilitating forms. Being anxious is, however, a part of our natural human state. We all need a certain level of psychological and emotional arousal for us to be both alert to dangers, and to motivate us into action that could ensure our survival. However, in modern times we don't have the same threats to life as our primitive ancestors did, and yet we are still primed to respond to our present-day threats—whether real or imagined—as if they were potentially life-threatening.

We all share some of the same basic anxieties—such as wanting to be liked and accepted by others, or wanting to be seen as 'good-enough' by other people. Some of us raise our state of anxiety far beyond this though, and we then create additional anxieties for ourselves, which lead to a more generalised fear and panic, and consequently to the behaviours fruitlessly designed to keep us safe in a seemingly unsafe world. We then have a toxic form of anxiety that is fuelled by our thoughts, and adversely affects our emotional balance and our ability to think clearly or rationally. Anxiety hijacks our primitive brain, which hasn't sufficiently evolved to be able to independently control our thoughts or emotions, and we set up a viscous circle that we become trapped within.

We can have a genetic predisposition towards anxiety, as well as then having had early childhood experiences that have caused us to become more hyper-alert and hyper-vigilant to any potential threats. Our brain actually treats any threat that we are vividly imagining as if it were real, and it signals to our body to respond and react—to either fight the opponent, or to escape from the threat; or else to play dead—like an animal that has realised that it has no chance of escape or of winning a fight. We create these powerful imaginary threats and if we don't learn more about them and how to change the patterns we have set up we are destined to keep recreating the dramas that give us the anticipated and guaranteed pay-off of even more anxiety.

Being anxious activates a part of your brain, that with prolonged activation, remains over-aroused. It can then be very difficult to calm down the mind and body. In such an emotional state, self-help books, affirmations and positive messages on your fridge magnets will have no effect upon you whatsoever. The body must be calmed down before the emotional, or limbic part of the brain can allow itself to be regulated and soothed. The first step involves *emotional regulation*, as we learn to soothe and rebalance our physical and then our emotional state. Then we need information, and the understanding of how this links into our own life experiences; and then essential skills-training, and only then will we see the tangible and ongoing changes we desire.

There can be physical causes of anxiety that no amount of talking therapy will change. If your body and mind are in a state of arousal due to a physical or chemical imbalance, or due to food sensitivities, or pathogens, then of course talking therapies and anxiety-reducing medications will not bring you any significant benefits. If your anxiety stems from your pre-verbal life—before the age of 3 years—it will be held and stuck in your body; and again no talking will reach this pre-verbal experience. Similarly, if your base-line of anxiety has been set too high due to your experiences in the womb, and/or your actual birth experience, and/or the way in which you were handled and cared for as a small infant then these too will not be adequately processed, understood or released by talking or by taking drugs, either prescribed or otherwise.

The way in which you 'talk-to-yourself' in your own inner world greatly affects not just your moods but the life you then create for yourself. You are what you think (and consume). It is therefore vital to learn how to change these negative internal comments and dialogues.

Accumulated anxiety finds many outlets such as in obsessive and compulsive thoughts and behaviours; in panic attacks; and in phobias. We may also adopt certain behaviours which we think or hope will help us, such as self-harm, addictions, and problematic relationships with food. Anxiety, when out of our control takes over, and has the capacity to ruin the quality of, our lives. We therefore owe it to ourselves to take back control; to find out the source(s) of our own anxiety, and most importantly to find effective treatments that don't involve putting alien substances into our bodies—artificial chemicals which then give us the added burden and arousal of having to detoxify them from our bodies. Our own empowering knowledge and skills are crucial to a balanced and enjoyable life. There is plenty of research which now supports the efficacy of methods such as visualisation, mindfulness, natural nutritional and herbal supplements, conscious breathing, and revising our unhelpful ways of thinking.

> Remember the **A-B-C** and **T-T-T** of emotional over-arousal:
>
> **A**drenalin Alert—**B**reath slowly and deeply—**C**alm down the body……..you can then begin to:
>
> **T**hink about what you need—**Ta**lk to yourself in a positive and soothing way, as you would to your own child—**T**reat your anxious body and mind with the natural herbal and nutritional supplements needed to help it to re-balance. A 'quick-fix' for anxiety is from the natural substance GABA—which can be bought on-line—and herbal remedies such as Kava Kava, Passiflora and Valerian.

Should you decide to attend this workshop module you will also learn about the many causes of anxiety, the types and levels of anxiety, and explore the anxiety in your own life as well as finding out several other important ways to regulate this state of emotional over-arousal and to thereby live a calmer and more balanced life.

Understanding Depression

Depression is a blanket word used to label or diagnose what is actually a wide range of symptoms and experiences. Depression can range from a more temporary and mild flatness of mood, which we all experience at some time, and which may be linked to a particular situation, disappointment, or hormonal imbalance. At the other end of the scale we see clinical depression in which the body/mind appear to be in a state of collapse and withdrawal from 'normal' life and the ability to carry out daily functions. There are many causes of depression, as well as several types of depression; and many possible treatments available too.

You may have inherited a genetic predisposition to having a lowered mood; and your early childhood experiences may well have reinforced this too. You may have learned to become hopeless and helpless instead of being more robust and resilient. Your mother's emotional state would have had a profound effect upon her ability to tune into your needs or to adequately meet them for you. You may then have been dependant upon someone who was not able to care for you in a way that you needed. The degree of love that you felt from others would have had a direct effect upon the way in which your brain became 'wired-up'. The body chemicals associated with both love or stress carve out their own particular neuronal pathways in a child's brain, affecting its very development and functioning.

We tend to think of depression as being an under-working, or a collapse, of the brain and body; but in fact, particularly where anxiety is associated with it, the brain is over-worked. Emotional areas of the brain are linked up to one another and over-arousal in one area then has a knock-on effect upon the next area, and a form of depression can follow. Poor sleeping patterns then make matters worse as the body and brain are not replenished sufficiently by the recuperative sleep that we all need each night. As you might be aware, chemical imbalances in the neurotransmitters of the brain result in mood and behavioural changes. Stress, inadequate nourishment—particularly a lack of proteins, specific minerals and vitamins—and dehydration all play a major part in these imbalances; as do our own perceptions, internal dialogue and thought processes.

Fortunately there are several things we can do to improve depression. Something as simple as 'dressing for success'—that is wearing clean smart clothes—has been shown to make a significant difference to how we feel and how we face the world. We may not feel like making an effort to help ourselves but it really does help!

It is important when working to change depression to also include changes to the level of energy within the body, and to use movement to shift this and to lift the mood and improve the overall outlook on life. Research has shown tangible benefits from doing certain activities, both individually and as part of a larger social and/or community group. For instance voluntary work helping other people, exercise and physical work, creative projects, music and comedy, learning new things both cognitively and experientially, and focussing upon the gratitude you have for the positive things—no matter how small—that you do experience each day. When we take our focus away from ourselves and the negative aspects of our lives we can then shift our energy and raise our vitality. Any distractions from our negative situation and feelings should be positive distractions—and not just involve spending money, or putting on another mask, or indulging in promiscuous encounters; all of which will only bring us more negative consequences, and further lower our energy and mood.

Just attending the module from 'The Ripple Effect' Process and learning something new will help you to change your experience of depression, because your brain is then processing the information it is receiving, and relating it to yourself; which takes the hard work and focus away from the emotional part of your brain. As we learn more about our emotions and moods, and the vital things we can do to improve them, we have a different energy, perspective, and self-concept. We can even learn how to change the inner dialogue that would otherwise hold us down in the pit of doom and despair which may have become our default position.

We are no longer hopeless or helpless unless we chose to be. Such a life-limiting choice may have previously become established because we expected to receive a secondary gain from the identity of being a depressed person, and the care and attention we could elicit from others because of this. If this is the case we need to find a way to take care of our own adult needs and not be manipulating others into taking care of us.

We should firmly take hold of the reins of our lives. We must find out if our depressed mood is due to physical causes and if so, to then rebalance the deficits and excesses—particularly deficits in our levels of Magnesium, Omega 3, and B-complex vitamins—and to rid the body of any pathogens which have been depleting our energy levels. We must commit to include regular uplifting events in our lives to give us something to look forward to, which includes spending time with lively energising people.

If you were to attend this workshop module you can expect to learn about the many causes and expressions of depression, and to explore the role that depression plays in your life; as well as finding out about the natural ways in which you can ease your symptoms of depression and find the path to a more energised and balanced emotional life.

"Numerous surveys have conclusively found that higher levels of education have a positive correlation with better health and a longer life, and even protect an individual from depression."

from The Art of Happiness by
HH Dalai Lama and Howard Cutler

Understanding Anger

Our anger is usually linked to our fears and the perceived threats to our well-being in some way; although it can also be a cover-up for our deeper sadness. Anger shows itself in a range of ways, from the bottled-up and internalised anger that can harm you both physically and emotionally, through to the out-of-control rage—which can understandably induce fear and anger in other people too.

We do need the ability to be angry and to show this at those times when we need to protect what matters to us; but what we don't want is to be like a volcano ready to erupt at even the slightest provocation. Anger has been necessary for our survival since primitive times, for instance if our camp were under attack and our tribe were being threatened with rape and death, we needed our anger and rage to energise us to fight and protect ourselves. Our anger quickly energises and empowers us and if we can learn to be its master, and to show it appropriately, it will be a useful ally against future threats.

Unfortunately in our modern stressful world we are surrounded by threats, whether real and potentially life-threatening or, more usually, only imagined to be so. Our brains are still primitive in some respects and if not 'up-dated' with new learning and skills we will be driven to react and behave in primitive ways—often with very bad consequences.

We all have our own personal history of anger—how it was shown in our family and by whom, whether it was allowed to be expressed, and the effects it has had upon our own sense of power or safety. Children who have not been shown the love, care and attention they need and deserve become angry with this deficit and injustice. Accumulated rage boils, bubbles and churns away under our socially acceptable surface, and it can burst free with either the right personal trigger, or the use of substances such as alcohol or drugs—which affect our ability to inhibit its expression.

Angry parents pass on their anger—together with fear—to their children; and we owe it to ourselves and to society in general to challenge and change the place that anger has held in our lives. Anger keeps us as its prisoner and we cannot expect a happy calm and rewarding life if anger still has a large part to play in it. We need to understand the purpose of our anger, and to find the knowledge and skills to put it in its place and for it only to surface when summoned.

What is your own relationship with anger? Where might this have come from? Where do you now feel and perhaps store anger in your body? Can you differentiate between your different levels of anger and how each one feels? Is your anger valid in the particular situation, or is it just a cover-up for something else? Does other people's anger scare you and cause you to withdraw, or does it enrage you?

Bashing cushions and screaming at the moon will not help you to understand, regulate or balance your anger.

Instead, in this workshop module you will find out how to calmly get back into the driving seat of your life and to take your foot off the anger pedal; to change to a lower gear and to cruise along admiring the scenery and enjoying the journey. You can become an advanced driver showing respect for yourself and towards other road users, who may well have their own faulty driving skills. You can then also teach others by example, how to be more calm, realistic, considerate and compassionate too.

"There are many different negative emotions….but out of all of these, hatred and anger are considered to be the greatest evil, because they are the greatest obstacle to developing compassion and altruism, and they destroy one's virtue and calmness of mind…….we need to actively cultivate the antidote to anger and hatred; patience and tolerance…… under rare circumstances some kinds of anger can be positive….when motivated by compassion or a sense of responsibility….where it can be used as an impetus or a catalyst for a positive action."

Dalai Lama—The Art of Happiness

How to Calm Down and Think Straight

We know that the mind has two distinct aspects—the conscious and sub-conscious; and that these play separate roles in our everyday lives. Our conscious mind is associated with our ability to plan, evaluate consequences, make judgements, and reflect upon the past; whereas our sub-conscious mind is primarily focussed on running the show, and includes the regulation of our bodily systems, and the computer-like hard-drive functions that have been 'programmed' in our early years, and it follows these diligently, making our outer reality fit with our sub-conscious belief system (for more information see www.qpp.uk.com Quantum Psyche Process). I believe that the conscious mind is then also sub-divided into two parts. There is a part that flits about and a part that is focussed. I see the first part as resembling a pony that hasn't been broken in and which trots or gallops around at will. The other part I see as the rider, who firmly grips the reins, sits upright and who then confidently rides the horse in the desired direction. Left to its own devices, the mind will randomly make links and associations and take the thoughts off into areas that I call 'Trivia and Trash'. Trivia is the stuff that does have an actual link to our lives, whether present, past or future; but it is trivial, irrelevant and superfluous. The Trash is just that—rubbish that our minds grab hold of and play around with—it serves no useful purpose and just wastes our time and energy. This is different from the free-flowing, creative, intuitive and dream-like aspects of the mind, which serve us well when allowed some time to play around and then to offer us solutions, ideas and images with which we can create something solid—which happened to me several times in the creation and development of 'The Ripple Effect' Process, and more recently Quantum Psyche Process.

In order to tame the wild horse and to sit comfortably in the saddle, we must increase our understanding of the process and learn the skills needed to both make this happen and for it to become sustainable.

Perhaps our own childhood experiences have left us unable to regulate and calm our own emotional state and our bodies carry the weight of emotional neglect or trauma. We can learn to change this by accessing the right hemisphere of the brain—which was dominant in childhood and which benefits from the use of imagery and metaphor—as well as by utilising the strengths of the left hemisphere of the brain when learning new ways to perceive and understand what we come into contact with, to communicate more clearly and effectively, and to assert our new boundaries. In these ways we reduce our current levels of stress, and enhance our ability to be resilient to it, and we thereby improve every aspect of our well-being. We can also change our unhelpful habits and find new ways of relating to both ourselves and to others. Being able to use our conscious, thinking and rational mind to its best will have a positive effect upon how we think, feel, and of course, on how we then behave.

We must also learn how to calm the body—which is essential before you can calm the mind; and I want to share with you an acronym I have created for you to use when you need to get to sleep.... BEER—no visual, olfactory or taste associations with the alcoholic beverage is intended! When we have difficulty getting off to sleep, despite following all the common-sense advice that abounds, what we really need is to get our bodies and minds into the zone associated with sleep. You may have to repeat this process a few times as the galloping pony will inevitably try to run away with your thoughts— so persistence is essential, as it is with everything else you want to accomplish in your life.

> **B.....Breath** slowly and deeply, into the back of your throat—which tricks the brain into thinking that you are on the cusp of sleep.
>
> **E....Eyes** closed and looking downwards level with the end of your nose—this is the 'off' position for the brain which you may have noticed if you read in bed and fall asleep whilst doing so. If your eyes, when the pony gallops around, rise up again as if looking upwards, then just bring them down and intend to keep them at that lower level.
>
> **E....Empty** your mind of thoughts, ideas, memories or plans....as best you can. On your outgoing breath imagine that the breath blows away any such thoughts—like gusts of wind blowing away fallen leaves from your garden path, leaving it clear.
>
> **R....Relax** your body, as if soaking in a warm bath; or sunbathing.... feeling the warmth penetrate every cell of your body, leaving you deeply relaxed, submissive and safe.

It is said that happiness equates to a calmness of mind, and now you will have the opportunity to create that for yourself.

If you are intrigued enough to find out more, then this workshop module will give you an understanding of what it is to be mindful, or to be an observer of your own life; as well as an increased awareness of how you have until now developed a lack of calmness in your thinking and emotional life. You will also learn new skills that will enable you to both regulate your stress and emotional arousal as well as understanding, challenging and changing your negative thinking patterns and inner dialogue, and their effects upon you. Furthermore you will gain an insight into the role of your imagination, and ways to use it to your advantage, and to have a new focus for meditation, and a new, more beneficial 'default' position for your brain to return to when not being consciously focussed upon a task. Calming the mind enables us to think straight and to take control of our life.....to tame the wild pony and to trot along at our own intended pace.

How to Play and Have Fun

People with gaps find it hard to play. Instead of showing our shame at this difficulty, we say that play is silly, childish and demeaning, and that it is something we have outgrown. The truth is that playfulness is never outgrown. It adds vitality to our lives and enhances our creativity, and our attractiveness in the eyes of others. Over the years, we may have had to develop a persona which wears a stern, serious or superior mask; and also to don the associated heavy costume, or suit of armour, in order for us to convincingly play out that part. In doing so we haven't developed our own script or learned how to present a genuinely fun and playful performance that is really our own.

We now know, from plenty of relevant research studies, that laughter and an optimistic and light attitude to life actually heals illness, disease and physical trauma. Yet it can seem alien to us to live like this. If we can recapture the playfulness of the child we once were—before things changed and playing had to end—we can reignite our vitality and playfulness, and greatly help our bodies and minds to function better and serve us well for longer.

As well as the significant health benefits of laughter and play, which are now well documented; an essential benefit of being more playful is that it enables you to connect with your own child(ren) and grandchild(ren) on a much more profound level. Raising children is the most important 'job' in the world and having the capacity to be spontaneous, light and playful makes a big difference in this.

So how can you have more playfulness in your life? Well you can 'see the world through the eyes of a child' from time to time—at least every day—and imagine removing the fears, doubts and responsibilities that hold you down so much of the time. Perhaps imagine people you have difficulty with as being colourful cartoon characters, or at least that they are wearing wacky fancy dress, and so lighten your interactions with them and the power you give them to affect your moods. If you regularly 'check-in' with the child inside you and ask what he/she wants and needs right now, you will not only be able to find your own way to meet that need, but it will free up your spontaneity as you won't need to constrain and silence your inner child any longer. Making time for creative hobbies helps to get us into the peak experience of 'flow', when we are totally absorbed in a project and time passes very quickly. This frees up the brain to work in better ways and to access a more intuitive and creative approach to life's challenges. Mixing with playful spontaneous, and yet still well-balanced and grounded, people also helps us to become more loose and playful ourselves. The many 'Meetup' groups around the country can help you to find like-minded people with whom you can share a new or existing interest. (See www..meetup.com)

If you are aware that your inability to play and bond with people is blocking your life in some way then this workshop module will help you to explore your lost or hidden playfulness, and reveal what has been blocking you; as well as preparing your body to loosen up and to allow itself to become more spontaneous, playful and to have fun in the safety of a small group.

"Laughter is a form of positive emotion that can influence your brain, heart, and blood-vessel function."

> Daniel Amen (American clinical neuroscientist and psychiatrist.)

"If we took what we know about the medical benefits of laughter and bottled it up, we would require FDA approval."

> University of California professor Lee Berk.

How to Balance Your Mind, Body and Weight

I am not interested in the simplistic and naïve approach to overweight that talks only of dieting, calorie counting or exercise. Instead I am much more interested in your relationship to your own body; how any imbalances in your body and brain lead to problems with your eating patterns and your weight; and most importantly, how to rectify these imbalances and have a healthier relationship with food and with yourself. Your present relationship with food may have been set up when you were a child. Maybe the family dinner table was a place of strict routines and expectations, and you have associated eating with certain negative emotions. Perhaps instead you didn't eat as a family but in secret isolation and you too, like me, had to steal or grab any food that you could find; or maybe you were kept quiet and distracted by food during your parents' absence. Food is so much more than just food for most of us, and we hoard it or reject it because of our own psychological and emotional connections to it. How you feel about our body, and whether you want to healthily nourish and take care of it, or not, will also be part of the mix.

There are many more causes of being overweight and obese than simply eating too much food and exercising too little. There are many factors that affect the subtle balance of your hormones, blood-sugar levels, your tendency to store fat and your ability to release and burn it. Not least of which is the consumption of heavily processed food with chemical additives which are alien to our bodies and place a huge burden upon our health.

It is time for a more holistic and comprehensive approach to the problems of excess weight and the associated health problems this creates for so many people. If we can take proper care of our bodies, and keep our bodily systems in balance, this then frees us all up to have healthier lives with the energy we need to function well, and it also allows us to take on new challenges and enrich our lives in new ways.

Our brains have been neglected when it comes to looking at our eating and weight problems. Instead we are constantly warned and advised about what to do to change our behaviours, whilst overlooking the motivations and neuro-biological needs which underlie the choices we make, as well as the addictive effects of much of the so-called 'food' on offer to us. Our choices affect our overall lifestyle and the quality of our lives, our health and ultimately our life-expectancy.

When we have the baseline of our physical health and well-being in order, this frees us up to properly address the next levels up, namely our emotional energy, our cognitive mental energy and will-power, our connection to loving relationships, and our more creative, intuitive and spiritual aspects. Having a healthy body greatly enhances our chances of having a healthy mind. Robust health underpins our higher levels of being. It is hard to live a lighter and more spiritually inclined life if your physical body is struggling to function; if your body is suffering from the effects of inflammation; if your body systems are out of balance and negatively affecting one another; if your immune system is under-working and not adequately protecting you, or even attacking your body itself because it doesn't recognise the mutated cells and alien organisms that it encounters there.

Most people eat whilst in a trance-like state, unaware of each mouthful or even the taste of the food being eaten. In the privacy of our own homes we usually guzzle down something, as quickly as possible, that takes away either our genuine feelings of hunger, or we try to fill up the feelings of emotional hunger, without being consciously focussed upon what we are doing. We stuff down sugar-filled artificial 'food' which makes us crave more sugary snacks—sugar is the mother of all addictions! If there was only one piece of advice I could give to anyone about food it would be to avoid refined carbohydrates. It isn't real and nourishing food. It messes up your body systems in far too many detrimental ways!

There is a relatively new and highly effective approach to health and well-being called Functional Medicine which informs this module of 'The Ripple Effect' Process. It addresses the deeper underlying causes of ill-health rather than the superficial conventional approach of diagnosing symptoms and treating them separately with drugs—which can create much greater problems, (whilst also making huge profits for the drug companies of course!) Functional medicine looks for the first domino that sets off the chain reactions in our bodies leading to the symptoms we finally express. (For more information please see the individual works of doctors Jeff Bland and Mark Hyman—both based in the U.S.A.)

There will be a lot for you to 'digest' if you attend this four-hour workshop and it will certainly nourish your mind. You can expect to find out about the many and varied reasons for being overweight; to learn about a great many food facts that you did not know; to understand how your brain is involved with your eating style and the ways in which you can balance your brain and body systems, which will in turn regulate your weight; how to improve your relationship with your body and with food; and how to eat consciously and with heightened awareness of the process and its consequences for your body and mind.

The following six modules of 'The Ripple Effect' Process are the groups that run for two hours a week for eight weeks. I have avoided giving any 'tips' in them simply because we as individuals, as well as the modules, are each too complex for brief snippets and advisory tips. Well-meaning but misplaced quick-tips can be as useful as a sticking plaster over a gaping bleeding wound.

Understanding Yourself

We are all unique and complex. We all have our own mixture of genes, in-utero and birth experiences, our own upbringing—and what we have learned to believe about ourselves from that—and our own set of positive and negative influences from the many people who have impacted us in our lives. No one theory exists that fits everyone's history and the ways in which our own personality has developed. We all go through life with our gaps in the essence of who we are and we have very little opportunity to really understand what has shaped how we have turned out as adults. We will have spent many years at school, college and perhaps university—but how much of that time was spent on learning about yourself? You may have degrees in academic subjects and yet know very little about your relationship with yourself and with other people, even though these are fundamental to a happier life. We need to learn much more than simply how to acquire a skill or trade, which we can later exchange in return for money—income that we then spend trying to feel better about the lives we have ignorantly created for ourselves.

Ask yourself;

> What do I really think and feel about myself?
>
> How do other people see me and what do they say about me?
>
> How compassionate am I towards myself?
>
> What kind of friend am I to myself?
>
> In what ways am I still affected by the negative influences upon me from my past?

If you don't like your honest answers to these questions then it is time for you to better understand and befriend yourself.

Most of us grow up learning how to be convincingly false. We learn how to adapt to fit into the needs and requirements of our families. These are not usually positive adaptations and can leave us not really knowing who we are, what our own values and needs are, or how to live a more authentic life on our own terms. The love, care and attention you received as a small child has determined your ability to form emotional attachments; which in turn greatly influence all of your relationships, and consequently your self-esteem, value and worth.

With the right guidance we can explore how our own family backgrounds have moulded us into who we are today, and how this affects every aspect of our current lives. Realising the ways in which the influences of our childhood subsequently influence our decisions and behaviours today is crucial to changing and enhancing the way we live.

Learning how to unblock your life, gain emotional balance, mental clarity and a greater awareness of your own needs will enable you to live your life to its fuller potential—not shackled to the past conditioning and programming of your family, and not having to wear a mask in order to be thought of as OK by other people.

Self-knowledge and awareness is both empowering and liberating. We can become free, authentic and the master of our own ship—in both the calm seas, and as we navigate safely through life's inevitable storms.

This eight-week group module will help you to find out much more about who you are, and why; and offer you information about child and personality development and the influences upon your brain's development; the role of emotional attachment and its effects upon many areas of your life; an understanding of how your own family system has shaped you and the decisions you have made about your life; the ways in which your authenticity has been squashed and the many ways that the 'false' self is expressed in your everyday life; greater self awareness, self-knowledge and improved emotional intelligence; as well as the opportunity to think about, explore and set your own personal goals based upon your new understanding and awareness.

Understanding Relationships

Magazines are regularly giving us advice from the so-called experts on our relationships, and also offering the quick-fix tips that we apparently need to give our relationships a much-needed boost. No psychological theory can ever truly fit the unique experience of the ongoing drama of a relationship—be that at work, with your extended family, or closer to home in your own family and with your partner/spouse. There are some commonly agreed aspects that make up a healthy and vibrant relationship—which unfortunately account for only the minority of relationships—as well as those that indicate when a relationship is chronically unhealthy or dis-eased. What is not usually covered is the way in which your brain affects not only your choice of partner but also the ways in which you then behave within your relationships.

Your ability to feel a loving attachment to someone, the ease with which you can feel and show intimacy, and the sort of person you are attracted to are all influenced by your own history and childhood experiences.

Most of us fell into relationships in our teens and twenties by default, or at best from a starting point of lust. Others focus their search for a relationship that will offer them that all elusive sense of security—which they will never find whilst they are looking outside of themselves. For those with less freedom of choice they may have felt pressured—either through family expectation or pregnancy—to form a relationship with someone they would not have chosen for themselves.

All relationships have a life-span and a series of stages—albeit not necessarily explicit or fixed—through which we have to navigate, and then perhaps re-negotiate the basis of the relationship, which sometimes leads to an ending of one sort or another. Knowing who we are as individuals, and finding ways to meet our own needs, and to regulate our own emotions frees us up to have more meaningful, intimate, honest and rewarding relationships, free from game-playing and manipulation.

Our relationships offer us the opportunity to learn the most about ourselves—with that particular person in that particular set of circumstances. We may succumb to the invitation to offload to our circle of friends about what is wrong with our relationships but this will not bring us the insight, or skills, to enable us to make any changes we want and need. Most of us didn't learn anything at school about what relationships really are and how to create and nourish them—and yet our relationships are crucial to our emotional survival and well-being.

Ask yourself;

Which of my relationships enrich my life and help me to grow as a person?

Which ones would I like to change, improve or discard?

Are my relationships similar to the ones I saw around me when I was growing up? If not, how are they different?

Do I avoid longer-term relationships? If so, why?

Do relationships scare or confuse me? If so, why?

What does a good healthy relationship look like?

Men are.........

Women are.................

What changes could I make to myself that would enable me to have better relationships?

The answers to these questions will no doubt open up more questions for you, and in turn this may stir up your curiosity and enthusiasm to find answers for yourself.

If you want to find out much more about relationships and the part they play in your life, then attending this eight-week group module will enable you to learn what a good, healthy relationship looks like; to find out how your individual styles of attachment and associated brain functioning affects your relationships; to discover the different levels of intimacy, and how to keep yourself emotionally soothed and regulated—which will make you available to be truly intimate; to explore love, attraction and compatibility; to discuss the stages of a relationship and the 'why and how' of endings; as well as to consider how your own improved relationships will enhance your life.

How to be More Confident

Feeling 'not good enough', or the object of the negative judgements of others, seriously restricts our enjoyment of life and even our ability to fully engage with life and the situations and people that we will encounter. We may have a genetic predisposition to being cautious, timid and fearful; but it is our subsequent upbringing that will either reinforce or change this for us.

Even if our lack of self-esteem and self-worth is long-standing and ingrained it is never too late to make some significant changes and improvements. When in the grip of social anxiety we cannot think clearly or realistically, and we cannot formulate what we want to say, or to express ourselves effectively. We can become paralysed as if trapped in the headlights of someone else's stare and their opinions about us.

Working to change this by making purely cognitive and behavioural changes doesn't address the vulnerable emotional part of who we are—a part that needs to feel safer and more confident in its ability to think and speak clearly, and to have its voice understood, respected and calmly responded to by other people.

For those people with a shaky sense of their own self-worth, value and esteem, making up lies, fictitious accounts and anecdotes seems like a good way to paint a better picture of themselves in the hope that this just might cover up their gaps and convince others of their worth and value. However the high risk of being exposed as a fraud, and having to suffer the humiliation that this would bring, gnaws away at them and raises their anxiety levels even further. We all tell lies to ease our own discomfort, or with the intention of reducing someone else's discomfort with a truth, or with something they might find shame-inducing. (Shame has been called the *master emotion* for its ability to swallow us up and render us worthless in our own eyes and, we imagine, the eyes of others). These sort of lies are on a different level to the pathological lies of the narcissist or psychopath—who both have little or no empathy for others, and who assume the position of "You don't matter and so it's OK for me to lie to you."

Some people are just 'difficult' to be around, for many reasons, and we need particular insight and skills to enable us to deal with them effectively—whether that be at home, at work, at college or university, or indeed anywhere where we cannot just avoid them altogether. As we learn new skills and become more assertive and better able to understand and communicate with others, we can take up our rightful place in the cockpit of our lives, confidently flying our plane through the storm clouds, and not just trembling with fear, unable to take off or terrified of crashing.

Ask yourself;

> What people or situations threaten my sense of self-worth? How do I then react?
>
> Do I fear being really seen and known by other people? If so, why? What might others discover about me that I find so worrying?
>
> If I did have a healthy and robust self-esteem, how would this change my life? What would I be doing differently?
>
> Have I ever witnessed a calm grounded and assertive person communicate with other people? How different is this to the ways in which I behave?

Very few of us have a stable and consistent sense of our own worth, value and competence. We are all a 'work in progress'—some people are further on than others, but we are all still journeying to self-improvement. We just need the right guidance, advice and opportunities—at the right time—to help us to develop into who we can, and who we deserve to be.

By attending this eight-week module you will give yourself the opportunity to understand the roots of low self-esteem; the labels you have been given—which you may still be holding onto; the 'programming' that you continually run which reinforces your sense of inferiority; as well as an understanding of what assertive behaviour really is, and how and when to use it; how to deal with difficult people; the different levels and styles of communication and their appropriate contexts; and how to have better 'contact' with yourself and with others.

'The Ripple Effect' Process

<u>How to be Happier</u>

Something that most of us share is the desire to be happy, or at least happier than we are. Few of us know what would actually make us happy let alone how to sustain this elusive state. The good news is that research has been carried out in recent years—linked to the 'positive psychology' movement—which gives us the answers we need and the ways in which we can not only become happier but also how to maintain this for ourselves over the longer term. This tells us that we all have a 'base-line' of happiness at any given time in our lives, and that this derives from our earlier experiences, the sense and meaning we have given to these, and the extent to which we have allowed them to affect our present lives. The good news is that this base-line amounts to only 50% of our total capacity for happiness. A further 10% is circumstantial and the remaining 40% is within our power to find, develop and integrate into our lives!

We now know what activities actually enhance our happiness, and the ways in which we can increase our own personal experience of happiness. This is definitely not linked to any dippy-hippy notions but is backed up by scientifically validated research. Firstly we need to be clear about what blocks our own sense of happiness, joy and contentment. These blocks will, of course, be unique to our personal history and experiences, and the meaning we have given to such experiences; and how they confirm our deeper core beliefs about ourselves and what we believe we deserve. When we have uncovered our own blocks we can then find ways to replace them with alternative life-enhancing perceptions, thoughts, feelings and behaviours.

Many of the people I have worked with over the years have been living their lives as if stuck in their past with their old out-dated thoughts, feelings and behaviours still determining their lives today—and consequently holding them back from a fuller richer life. Perhaps they have had to be the 'caretaker' for other family members and in doing so have sacrificed their own dreams, ambitions and relationships; maybe they have experienced trauma and abuse in their past and they still allow this to dominate their present-day life; it might be that they are in an empty relationship which is devoid of any emotionally intimate connection. There are many ways and reasons to feel unhappy. There are also many fruitless ways in which people try to cover-up their sadness, such as with buying 'stuff' they do not need; or by being constantly busy with new projects, responsibilities or a full social calendar; or chasing fame and celebrity only to find that their sadness still hangs around them like an unwanted shadow.

Ask yourself;

> When am I at my most happy and contented?
>
> What gets in the way of my happiness?
>
> Do I know any people who are genuinely happy and contented?
>
> Do I mix with happy people? If not, why?
>
> Where in my body do I experience and carry my sadness, and my happiness? How different do they feel?
>
> Am I worth the effort it will take to increase my baseline happiness and to maintain it? If not, why?

As well as your own individual experiential rewards you can also expect this eight-week module to offer you; an understanding of the happiness you are missing out on and what you could attain; the ways in which you can do this by learning new 'happiness-enhancing' skills, changing your outlook on life, and developing a life which feels emotionally lighter, and which frees you up to live more in the present moment—which is really the only time you have; an opportunity to learn how your optimism, hope, forgiveness, kindness, gratitude, achievement of your realistic goals, social comparisons, social relationships, and care of your body-mind will all bring you greater overall happiness; and also to learn how to sustain these improvements and carry your new found happiness into your future.

UNDERSTANDING YOUR SUB-PERSONALITIES

It is important at the outset to make it clear that we all have sub-personalities and that these are not the same as having multiple personalities (also called Dissociative Identity Disorder—which is much more profound, and is clinically diagnosed as a form of mental illness). These can be seen as a small cast of extras who fill out our life-dramas. They can come on to the centre stage of your life either by your own direction, or they may instead burst forth independently and steal the show—not usually in a good way!

When we were young we would not have been able to make sense of many of the situations and experiences we had, and neither did we have well-developed verbal, cognitive, or reasoning skills back then. As a creative way of adapting to our circumstances we therefore developed sub-personalities. These sub-personalities were created as a survival mechanism—intended to shift the intensity of an ongoing experience onto one particular aspect of ourselves, and for us to then hold and contain those experiences within that sub-personality. We later built upon and expanded this new part and created certain behaviours and ways of speaking and reacting that we thought would be the best way of handling our difficulties at that earlier time in our lives. As young adults we may also have chosen to create and develop sub-personalities as an attempt to fill-in the gaps of our 'self' that we were becoming painfully aware of. Sadly this well-intentioned path is rife with its own potholes, because our immature sub-personalities don't have the ability to really help us out in our adult lives, and tend to get in the way of our being able to live an authentic and emotionally enriched life. Sub-personalities can instead add to our gaps. We may still be operating from old scripts with old characters in their well-worn costumes and with their well-rehearsed lines at the ready, but our life drama has inevitably changed since we were a child or teenager, and we need to learn more appropriate ways of staging our show and of presenting it every day with honesty and integrity.

We tend to assume that we are just one person, but if you think back you will no doubt recall incidences when you behaved in a way that was 'out of character' for you, or perhaps a persona appeared that took control and dealt with a situation in a way that you didn't think you were capable of. These are examples of our sub-personalities. Aspects of our overall self which wait in the wings of our lives in case we need them. We may not consciously intend them to show up, but our sub-conscious mind may beckon them on stage—along with their own script and body language—for them to then take on and play out the role for which they were created, and to make our external reality fit with our internal belief system. For instance, if you were in a new and unknown environment, such as being abroad in a country that you were not familiar with, how do you imagine you would tend to behave in an adverse or even a life-threatening situation?

Would you regress to being childlike and cry, or beg for help?

Would you relish the challenge, become energised, take charge and lead the way?

Would you be frozen with fear and incapable of finding a solution?

Would you flirt with anyone who might be able to get you out of there?

Perhaps you can only guess how you'd react in such a situation, but you will no doubt have similar real experiences to draw upon which will reveal some of your own sub-personalities which lie beneath the surface of your socially-acceptable persona.

Discovering and exploring our sub-personalities is a deeply experiential challenge. It would be very helpful to you to have first completed the eight-week module entitled 'Understanding Yourself' beforehand as a good starting point for then undertaking this deeper level of work. In this module you can expect to gain an awareness of your own sub-personalities and the roles they play in your life; how and why they do this (i.e. their purpose); to understand, and then be able to integrate those sub-personalities which still serve you well and enhance your life; and to be able to let go of those that have been blocking your progress and tripping you up so far.

UNDERSTANDING YOUR INNER CHILD

You were once a child. A child who was totally dependant upon those around you to show you love, to willingly give you the time you needed, to sensitively care for you and to meet your essential emotional and physical needs as best they could. We all needed to feel wanted and special. Most of us didn't, and the gaps started to be formed.

As small children we were all physically and emotionally/psychologically impacted by everything we experienced; by what we needed, longed for and even begged for—and particularly by what we didn't then receive. At this early age we all felt the intensity of our emotions and they shaped both the way in which our brains developed, and how we then coped with the life circumstances that we had been born into. We learned what was 'conditional' and what we had to do to be accepted and allowed to stay within our own family groups—no matter what it cost to our own emerging personal identity and sense of self-worth. If we had such conditions put upon our behaviour we will probably still be living with these nowadays. By conditions I mean the ones that begin..... "you should/must/ought to..... in order to be seen as OK and to be allowed to stay here with us." The conditions which said that in order to be given any attention you must behave in a certain way, and do—or not do—certain things. This is very different from a good parent's healthy unconditional guidance of their child towards socially and culturally acceptable behaviours, which would then protect the child by reducing the likelihood of the child feeling the implosion of shame for any perceived wrong-doings.

Lack of good-enough parenting shaped who you are, how you behave, and what you believe you deserve. Gaps caused by the wounds to your Inner Child will also show themselves as:

Difficulties with your emotional stability and your capacity to think and to express yourself clearly.

An insecure sense of your own value—finding it hard to like yourself and to show yourself love, empathy and compassion.

Difficulties in asking for what you want or need.

Problems with authority figures.

Difficulties with your sexual boundaries.

Your inability to be emotionally and sexually intimate.

A negative relationship to your own body and how you treat it.

Problems with your career progress.

Patterns of difficulties with all of your relationships, and your part in choosing them, staying in them and ending them.

So, a very wide range in which your fundamental gaps can show up in your life!

In my work as a psychotherapist I am less interested in the 'external' expression of the wounded Inner Child, such as the depth and length of self-inflicted cuts, scratches or burns; or the amount of calories consumed daily; or the amount of money spent either gambling or shopping; or the excess hours worked each week; or the hours spent looking at pornography. Instead I am more interested in what the Inner Child has experienced that has led to such attempts at mood-altering behaviours. If we only deal with the symptoms we don't reach the causes. We may change or remove a particular symptom—by using a cognitive-behavioural approach—but another symptom will probably soon appear to take its place and express the deeper pain once again. Your Inner Child carries the scars of your actual childhood experiences. This is the place where the wounds were made and it is the place of the greatest and most profound healing.

It can be easier for many of us to feel and show compassion for someone else's wounds than it is to acknowledge and soothe our own—yet we need and deserve our loving compassion too. Healing our own gaps enables us to be an example to others and to be able to offer and share genuine care and intimacy with others.

Not surprisingly, working at this level is deeply experiential and for this reason it is important to have done some preliminary work before attending this eight-week module—in the form of prior attendance at the 8-week group 'Understanding Yourself'. It may be tempting to dive into the hideout of your wounded inner child and to rush to help them—but the scared kitten will not come out from under the sofa if you make a grab for it.

This module is not suitable for those who have experienced serious and ongoing abuse, trauma and neglect, which would be better served by initially working one-to-one with a competent and sensitive psychotherapist, to access the intensity of any repressed thoughts, feelings and body sensations. Until this has been successfully completed this modules might not feel safe enough, or appropriate, for you to expose your vulnerable self to at this deeper level. When you do feel ready for this module you can expect to: access your own inner resources which will then enable you to work at this level; make safe contact with your Inner Child—at different ages; communicate with him/her and establish unmet needs; advocate on behalf of your Inner Child; and release some of the milder traumatic experiences which have been blocking your life until now.

We have now looked at the ways in which your gaps will be showing themselves in your life, and the ways in which you can bring about their healing through the process of learning, understanding, experiencing, sharing, integrating and changing. These are the foundations of the Psycho-Emotional-Education modules which make up 'The Ripple Effect' Process and they all have this purpose in mind.

I sincerely hope that the reading of this book will have been of some help to you, independently of whether you attend any of the modules or not. I have tried to include enough here to be of value, and yet perhaps encourage you to further explore yourself too.

In A Nutshell

I can still remember a few aspects of my annual visits to my grandmother when I was a child, and one of the things I clearly recall is her sitting at a small round table next to the window of her living room, so as to benefit from the daylight. She already wore glasses but she would then hold up a magnifying glass too, through which she would read from a hardback book—which had a deep purple cover jacket—entitled 'Enquire Within Upon Everything'.

Whilst I certainly don't presume to include 'everything' here, as that's clearly impossible, that book title has stayed with me over the years. Perhaps this is because I have always had a thirst for knowledge, although in my early years little chance to quench it and few opportunities to enquire about anything. The thought of enquiring within just one book and finding out lots of new things really appealed to me, even back then, and I still like encyclopaedias for this reason.

The relevance here, is that in this final part I want to present to you a wide range of articles that I have recently written, and have now adapted for this book. I wrote them at the suggestion of the young man who helped me to set up my websites, which have links to social media sites. He advised me to start writing articles for a 'blog' page for the website as a way of introducing my ideas to the public, and to spread the word of 'The Ripple Effect' Process and how it could be of help. I first began nervously, and soon became enthusiastic about writing articles for the 'blog'—something I had resisted and avoided up until then due to my lack of IT skills and what I saw as my inability to be a 'writer'. Prior to that time I'd imagined 'writers' to be intellectual folk who had attended private schools and were very familiar with classical literature—to the extent that they spouted quotations and character analyses whenever the opportunity arose—and they were also 'au fait' (pun intended) with Latin and French phrases, which they sprinkled liberally into their spoken and written words. (I've met a few psychotherapists like this too. What I judged to be their pretentiousness used to irritate me, but I now see that they are probably just trying to be seen by others as intellectually superior, which is a defence against the more real and deeper sense of inferiority that their own gaps bring them). I then knew for sure that I did want to write a book, to inform the public about 'The Ripple Effect' Process, and so I eagerly booked myself a place on a Writer's Workshop, held in early March 2012, to try and find out how to go about it. As it turned out undertaking the challenge of writing several articles has in itself proved really helpful to me in formulating my thoughts, experiences and ideas. These articles were also published on-line and have now been re-tweeted and reproduced elsewhere too—which has helped to validate to me their worth and relevance.

After they were added to the website for 'The Ripple Effect' Process—www.the-ripple-effect.co.uk,—and linked to my ongoing national advertising campaign for the project, I was invited to submit short snappy articles and brief visualisations for a national magazine—which I did, about 28 as I recall. I am now also including here some of these, which I hope you might find helpful. At the time I found it quite difficult to include much of value or depth in such short pieces of 200 words or less, but on reflection it was a good exercise for me in brevity—my friends would probably say that I do need that sometimes! These days all that is wanted by the media is "7 ways to....", or "5 things you should do ....." and so on. Just short tips and snippets. Has our attention span shrunk to the point at which we can only cope with bullet-points and 5-7 tips for a better life? Such national women's magazines usually include at least one set of self-assessment questions, requiring ticks in boxes and then the totting-up of a score from your answers to the 4-6 options available in each section. You are then told what 'type' of person you are from the responses you have given on that particular day, in the particular mood or mindset you were in at the time of the 'assessment'. I strongly dislike these 'let us tell you who you are' questions and evaluations. I find them simplistic, naïve, and lacking respect for the complexity and individuality of the reader. Yet they must be popular because they appear each month, covering the 'topic of this month's issue'. Such is the thirst for self-knowledge. Sadly it is trivialised and exploited by such popular magazines.

I begin with an article about Psycho-Emotional-Education, or PEE, as this is the basis of 'The Ripple Effect' Process and the 12 modules which comprise it. Then I talk about the power of groups which is again linked to the project too. After that come a mixture of topics most of which are not included within 'the Ripple Effect' modules at all, but which are still relevant and, I hope, will expand your knowledge and awareness in some meaningful way, and make the reading of this book worthwhile to you, whether or not you decide to attend any of 'The Ripple Effect' Process modules.

Our brains are constantly making links and associations. My brain makes a strong link between reading, and the holding of paper and the turning of real pages; and of flipping back to a previous page when my mind wanders and I have not been fully taking-in what I've been reading. I do not tend to read much on-line, and I have a short attention span when reading from a screen. I like to browse through bookshops, and I like a book that I can feel, smell, and carry with me to dip into when I make the time to enjoy doing so. I have asked friends what they thought about my on-line articles and almost all of them said that they didn't like reading from the internet, or that they didn't have the time to do so. Perhaps sharing these 'in a nutshell' articles, poems and visualisations with you as part of this book will give you the choice of reading them at your leisure, with a real page to be turned. If however, you are developing new associations between the written word and e-books, then you are ahead of me, and I hope that you enjoy the experience. Perhaps I'll try e-books and electronic reading devices myself one day.

PSYCHO-EMOTIONAL-EDUCATION.

You may not have come across this term before, but you can probably guess what it means.... educating people both psychologically and emotionally. It involves learning about what has shaped who we are and how we think, feel and behave. We do not have to be a slave to our history or conditioning—we can learn new ways to balance our thoughts and emotions, to understand why we behave as we do in particular situations and with certain people, and most importantly, how to change these things for the better. Understanding how our past has shaped us in the present day, and more importantly the choices we now have, and the changes that we can make, all serve to empower us as individuals and collectively as a society. As one person changes the ways in which they think, feel and relate to others; then others in turn are affected by those changes, and can also pass them on ....and so the ripple-effect expands.

We are accustomed to years of education at basic and advanced levels in many academic subjects; but very rarely will anyone have been educated about themselves. We reach adulthood not knowing why we are the way we are, or what we can do about it. Neither have we learned about inter-personal relationships and how they work, and why they don't; or about how to enrich our lives and ensure greater and sustainable levels of natural happiness. I believe that the ability to understand, take responsibility for, and to regulate, our emotional state is secondary in importance only to the acquisition of a healthy and robust self-esteem. Our parents, and earlier generations, will not have had any form of 'Psycho-Emotional-Education' themselves—and no-one can pass on to their children what they do not already know, or have, for themselves.

We are all complex beings with our own genetic make-up and innate tendencies, our own unique history, experiences, perceptions, preferences, and ways of expressing ourselves, and of getting our needs met, or not. We all experience a range of emotions—which inform us about what is going on for us in our personal 'inner-world', and which then motivate us into action. Firstly we perceive something, then we see, hear, smell and perhaps taste. We then very quickly think, imagine, and feel emotions and bodily sensations....and then we behave in a certain way—which is judged either positively or negatively.

When we can understand our emotions and behaviours we can shift the focus from the Emotional/Limbic area in our brains, to the brain areas which deal with making sense of things, planning and regulating our moods and behaviours, and enabling us to have a considered response rather than an emotional reaction to a person or an event. This process activates the more rational and sensible Adult inside us and helps us to calm and soothe our raw emotional Inner Child—the part which is still running our lives most of the time.

In creating the integrated programme of Psycho-Emotional-Educational modules which make up 'The Ripple Effect' Process; my aim has been to de-mystify therapy and to share with the public some of the relevant and effective theories, skills, techniques and ways of self-expression, and intra-psychic (me-with-me) and interpersonal (me-with-others) ways of relating. The modules all represent a brief, inexpensive and yet very effective method of building self-knowledge, empowerment and change, and they offer a relevant alternative to counselling, coaching or psychotherapy for many people. They can also represent a valuable addition to longer-term therapy for other people as they bring increased insight and awareness, and they offer the skills necessary to bring about real change! In order to make this P-E-E available to more people the cost has been kept very low. Attending all 12 modules would still cost less than a few months of personal therapy. Modules can be taken-up as single stand-alone units, or people can expand their knowledge and awareness further by attending as many as they wish.

The actual process of 'The Ripple Effect' comes in the form of small groups—with a maximum of six adult members. This small group size replicates a family-size unit and has been found to be the most safe, effective and beneficial way of working, learning and experiencing emotional change.

There are 12 'modules' in the programme, consisting of 6 workshops lasting for 4 hours each—called Understanding Anxiety, Understanding Depression, Understanding Anger, How To Calm Down And Think Straight, How To Play And have Fun, and How To Balance Your Mind Body And Weight. There are also 6 eight-week groups, of 2 hours per week; again with a maximum of 6 members attending. These modules are called Understanding Yourself, Understanding Relationships, How To Be More Confident, How To Be Happier, Understanding You Sub-personalities and Understanding Your Inner Child.

I have lost count of the number of new clients I have seen over the years who have told me that they had spent months or years, and a considerable amount of money, elsewhere in counselling; and yet they still had their initial underlying problem(s)! Talking about, and reflecting upon, your anger, anxiety, depression, lack of happiness and fulfilment, your sense of alienation, your relationship problems, your lack of confidence and self-esteem, your poor communication and relating skills, your weight and health problems, your addictions and dysfunctional behaviours; does not change them. We all need to gain an understanding of why we have such difficulties....and more importantly what we can do to bring about the changes we want and need.

'The Ripple Effect' Process group members are also all encouraged to keep in touch with one another, if they want to. This is a significant difference to 'therapy group' boundaries. We all need to 'belong' to a group of people who have had a shared experience...to feel that we have bonded and connected with others at a deeper and more meaningful level than the everyday chit-chat and gossip that most people fill up the space in their lives with.

One-to-one personal therapy is however preferable in cases of unresolved childhood trauma, abuse and/or neglect; or of a pronounced attachment disorder; or acute or prolonged-duration trauma disorder; and for certain personality disorders and some milder forms of mental illness. Personal therapy can be very useful for couples work too when the dynamic of the relationship becomes the 'client'.

Coaching has become a widespread business, both with life-coaching and business-coaching; and training courses vary greatly in their quality, depth and relevance. Coaching tends to be cognitively-focussed with the setting of goals and strategies for how to attain them—which are important aspects of any individual's adult life. However we are all much more than just our thinking minds. Coaching does not include working with the underlying reasons for our difficulties, and this may result in a re-occurrence of them, albeit in a different form: for instance we may be 'coached' into setting our goals and strategies for change in our work and business life, but without a deeper exploration of why we have created our difficulties in the first place, we are likely to repeat them and then create problems for ourselves elsewhere in our lives. We all have our own 'Life-Script' linked to our powerful sub-conscious mind-set. We have physical bodies, emotions, an Ego, an imagination, our thoughts and ways of expression, as well as our existential and trans-personal facets. We are integrated and comprehensive—and we need an approach to guidance and learning that is also integrated and comprehensive. P-E-E meets this need.

GROUP POWER

Any group, from a 3-person triad to a team, or a tribe, has a magnified effect upon its individual members as well as upon the outside environment in which the group exists. Group members become accountable to one another and can offer empathy and support; and this has been shown to result in greater focus and effectiveness of the group.

As a psychotherapist I am particularly interested in the therapy group; and, as the founder of 'The Ripple Effect' Process, I am also interested in the small group involved in learning and changing as a result of Psycho-Emotional-Education.

As soon as we are born we belong to a group—our family group. Later we may become members of other groups such as a religious group, an educational group, a peer group, a hobby-based group, a social group, a political group, a community-based group, and of course, a society, and a national group. As we mature we can choose those groups that we want to affiliate to. Those groups that we perceive as being similar to us in some significant way—perhaps through our interests, or our enforced and/or shared experiences.

In any group we cannot help but re-create our earlier experiences of other groups; such as in our families, or at school. We then overlay the present-day group with aspects from the past and react and behave 'as-if' we were still in that older experience. This may show itself as mistrust, shame or withdrawal; or alternatively perhaps as being pompous, arrogant, theatrical or over-bearing.

The group size is very significant. We can all 'hide' in a large group of 12 or more. Smaller groups of around 6 people become more intimate, intense, and thereby more rewarding as we become more attuned to others, and we involve ourselves more in the group— which becomes a separate entity in its own right and more than just the sum of its members.

A group takes on its own life if given the time and fertile ground in which to flourish. Safety is established by a respected and experienced group leader/facilitator—although challenges may well be made to this leadership during a group's lifetime. Having clear 'ground-rules' about what is, and is not, permitted, and having this agreed to by all members is crucial. Boundaries associated with time, venue, confidentiality, self-care and respect, also give a robust 'container' for a group.

The dynamics within a group are rich and inevitably varied. Everyone brings their own expectations, fears and needs. Everyone is trying to work out where they belong in the group and the role they will either assume for themselves, or that they will allow others to assign to them.

A group may witness in its members the emergence of several 'roles' in the group; such as a leadership-challenger, a 'top-of-the-class', a 'silent observer', an attention-seeker, a vocal 'hungry-chick' in the nest, a verbal 'sniper' and many other remnants of the past stories of the individual members. They will all subconsciously try to re-create their own 'past-story' within an ongoing group—either to reinforce the outcome of their 'script', or in the hope of changing the ending to a more favourable one for themselves. An experienced group leader will sensitively and firmly challenge these old-script behaviours and invite a more healthy and positive way of relating—with the added opportunity to actually try out new ways of being with, and relating to, the other group members.

A group leader must be able to maintain clarity between what is real and what is being imagined and 'projected' onto the group or onto an individual within that group. Being on the receiving end of someone else's 'projections' or 'transferences' onto you can be detrimental if these are simply accepted, unchallenged and absorbed 'as-if' they were real. Such acceptance of what others say about us is something we all did as children and it has shaped our self-concept ever since. We no longer have to accept any restricting judgements, labels, or opinions. Instead we can evaluate their truth about, and relevance to, the present-day situation; and we can now choose to reject and discard them, in a way that we couldn't do as a child. In a group we have the chance to check-out what is really 'me' right now, and what is just 'your stuff that is being dumped on me'. We can learn to monitor our own reactions and responses and to discard what doesn't 'fit' our actual experiences.

In a group we can also learn 'clean and clear' language—to say what we actually mean, with less chance of being misunderstood. Everyone passes what they hear through their own internal 'filter', which derives from their own childhood. This filter may well be defective and faulty. If so, communications will be distorted and changed to mean something else—something that 'fits' their own history and subsequent belief system. They will react 'as-if' this distortion were the truth. Such processing can be unearthed and changed within a safe group—which has a ripple-effect to the outside world of the group members' other relationships.

Group members' individual stories, and the sharing of emotions, can have a deep impact upon the listeners and can resonate with, and evoke, their own memories. Shared empathy and a knowing that someone else can understand our pain, fear and sadness can be a powerful healer—as long as the personal sharing is professionally facilitated and contained within the safety of the group. Enforced 'sharing' and even 'over-sharing' can have a detrimental effect upon everyone concerned!

Most groups will have a familiar dynamic of the Karpman Triangle going on. In this, there emerges a Vulnerable Victim, a Responsible Rescuer, and a Powerful Persecutor. The Victim elicits Rescue and then switches position and turns on the Rescuer and Persecutes them for having tried to rescue them. An alternative dynamic is a Rescuer looking for and setting up a Victim; and then switching to Persecuting that Victim instead of rescuing them. It is a common 'game' seen in families and in the workplace. You may not, at first, realise that this game is being set-up ..... and the only way out of it is to just not play the game! This can be harder than it sounds—as old ingrained habits, patterns and dramas can be difficult to expose and change.

The strength and safety of any group is a reflection of its leadership. All groups go through stages—from being formed (is it a group looking for a leader, or a leader looking for a group?); to setting up and normalising the group's ground rules and boundaries; to the dynamic interactions of group members; and the agreement of an ending process. In groups that have a specific purpose and agenda, such as in an educational or community group, these dynamics are restricted and tend to exist in the background. They are not addressed unless the group has a stated therapeutic purpose such as personal/spiritual development.

Group experiences from the 1970's and 1980's displayed looser boundaries and ground rules. There may well have been a focus on 'catharsis' or the overt—and perhaps compulsory—display of emotions such as anger/rage and sadness/despair and the obligatory sobbing. We now know that people grow and learn better in a safe and contained/boundaried environment, and that the customary 'cushion-thrashing' of yesteryear only reinforces the attachment to the behaviour and does not enable a person to make sense of their emotions or to balance and regulate themselves.

You cannot avoid belonging to a group—either actively or passively. Groups can be a powerful place in which to learn, change and grow; or they can keep you stuck in the identity of a group—such as in a self-help group where membership is dependant upon your being in need of the group's ongoing help and support.

With greater awareness, derived from a healthy group experience, you can become empowered to chose only life-enhancing groups in which to 'belong' in the future.

Is Therapy Right for You?

You won't know until you try it out, but if you work with the 'wrong' therapist for you, this will probably put you off ever finding a better one!

There is no point in even beginning counselling or psychotherapy if you cannot 'make use if it'. A competent therapist will be able to assess, very soon, whether you are 'psychologically available' to be able to make sense of and to integrate your work together, or not. If not they are ethically obliged not to exploit you if the work is unlikely to be of benefit to you. It would just be a waste of your time and money. This therapeutic assessment will consider your 'ego-strength'—which is your level of psychological resilience, or how stable you are and how much of the work you are likely to 'take-in' and use. People with profound personality disorders or chronic mental illness cannot generally derive much from counselling or psychotherapy—but some milder disorders may be helped. Your family, partner, or friends may recommend that you 'go for counselling'; but even though they probably mean well, they are not in a position to know if it is what you really need or not.

It is the relationship you form with the counsellor/psychotherapist which has been shown to be the most effective indicator of whether the work will be of benefit to you. But if you have a history of making bad relationship decisions, of having weak boundaries, of being manipulated, of being a people-pleaser, or you are just profoundly lonely and needing regular contact with a caring person; then you will not be in a place to accurately assess what is best for you, and who is the best therapist for you to work with.

Professional qualifications can be an indicator of a therapist's knowledge and skills, but this is not necessarily the case. Do you know what the letters after their name actually stand for? It may be a 3-6 year academic course of study, or only a brief introduction to counselling skills that they have completed. Similarly, the fees charged are not an indicator of quality either. An excellent therapist may be in a financial position to charge less than the 'going rate'; or an average counsellor may try to inflate their 'worth' with a high fee. Who you choose to work with says something significant about you too. We all 'project' onto other people some aspects that aren't really there.

If you don't want face to face contact with a therapist you can approach the Samaritans for free help, or other telephone or Skype counselling agencies, or individuals. Charity run 'befriending' agencies, and voluntary centres, may be free or very cheap, but these could still be a waste of your time and money.....with no change! Again this choice says something about you and how much you value yourself and your willingness to relate with someone on a deeper level, and the value you place upon your emotional health. I have known clients who spend large sums of money on gadgets/trinkets/smoking/drinking/holidays etc. and yet they can't 'justify' to themselves spending money to change their life from the inside. Some people would rather 'cover up' the outside with designer labels and a tan, than look beneath into their wounded soul.

If you want a counsellor/therapist to just 'sit and listen' to you then they are to be found too. If you want someone to challenge your thinking and behaviours, and help you to change you will need to find out if this is what is on offer.

A psychotherapist should have had a broader and wider training than a counsellor; and yet, still, psychotherapy trainings vary in their scope and relevance to the needs of the general public. Some trainings are 'cognitively' based and focus upon the client's thinking process; some are 'humanistic' and focus upon the emotional and relational aspects; whilst others are 'trans-personal' and spiritually inclined. Research has shown the efficacy of 'Integrative' psychotherapy which combines all of these aspects, and more. This approach has been shown to be the most effective way of working with a client and the wide range of issues that they bring into the therapist's office. To use an analogy of a car and garage; you wouldn't take your car to be fixed in a garage that had only one tool to use! Working 'integratively' with your psychotherapist will at the very least ensure that he/she has a few more tools at their disposal...just how many depends upon their commitment to ongoing learning and training. There are also specialists who work predominantly or exclusively with such presenting issues as Post-Traumatic Stress Disorder, refugee trauma, relationships, children, and the arts—such as play, drama and creative art work.

The following 4 levels of psychological difficulty and associated treatments may help you to see which best suits your present circumstances:-

Level 1
Temporary difficulties linked to an external event or situation, and a change or decision is sought. Time is wanted to explore a preferred outcome. (e.g. workplace problems; grief; life transitions.)
Treatment—short-term Counselling.

Level 2
Interpersonal (me-with-others) and Intrapsychic (me-with-me) relationships; mood disorders and self-esteem problems that may be masked by dysfunctional behaviours; traumatic event(s) and/or childhood issues that interfere with

present-day life; attachment and intimacy problems; difficulties with setting and maintaining limits and boundaries; pathological grief.

Treatment options—Psychotherapy, Quantum Psyche Process and 'The Ripple Effect' Process.

Level 3

Chronic and/or acute disturbance of personality and sense of reality; severe childhood trauma(s), abuse, and/or neglect; personality disorders including Multiple Personality Disorder (called D.I.D.); untreated chronic or acute Post-Traumatic-Stress-Disorder.; addictions to drugs, medications, or alcohol; lack of ego-strength or integrity.

Treatment—Long-term psychotherapy—preferably more than once a week.

Level 4

Brain-damage or organic retardation; profound mental illness; sociopathic/ psychopathic behaviour; severely disordered personality; sexual and/or violent criminality.

Treatment—Psychiatric services.

As you can see there are many levels of therapeutic help available and many reasons to seek a competent therapist to help you with these. I hope this article clarifies for you whether therapy would be right for you, and if so I wish you well in your quest, and hope that you make the changes you desire. Don't forget—it's the relationship that heals, but you still have to do your part and commit to the process, once you find the right person to work with. That will include you listening to your gut instincts, as well as to your head; and researching the therapist's training, qualifications, theoretical approach, and of course their fees, as well as how flexible they are willing to be about the time and frequency of your meetings, and for how long you might be working together.

Are You a Good Enough Parent?

The term 'Good Enough Parent' was coined many years ago by a psycho-analyst and pioneer in child development called Donald Winnicott (1896-1971). You cannot be a 'perfect' parent, as there is really no such thing; so 'good-enough' is good enough!

How you raise your child(ren) has a profound effect upon other people too, because your child's personality and behaviour has a 'ripple effect' to everyone else they encounter in later life.

Recent news stories have given us more shocking evidence of the lack of adequate parenting within our society. Children becoming overly-sexualised, and exposed to inappropriate images via TV, the internet, and in teen magazines; charities having to be set up to help feed children a nutritious breakfast before they start school; neglectful parents expecting schools to instil basic moral values into their pupils; children left indefinitely with relatives who torture and murder them in the name of 'casting out evil spirits'; young children whose whereabouts are unknown during the evening hours; parents not making time to read to, or talk with, their children. Parenting is THE most important job in the world—so how and why do we get it so wrong?

This is not a new phenomenon. When I worked in the Civil Service in the early 1980's I regularly encountered school leavers who could not even sign their name, and instead could only sign with a 'X' on their claim forms. They had no use-able skills, no future hopes or aims, little education and poor verbal skills. They will now be the parents, or even grandparents, of today! Poor parenting has been around for a very long time. Nowadays we have TV programmes dedicated to educating parents about how to raise their children. Sadly these programmes will not even be watched by the very people who need them most, and they would be a case of 'too little, too late' anyway.

The present British government is now piloting a project to improve parenting skills in the hope of avoiding future riots like those seen recently in many cities in the UK. It will take time to put right the deep-rooted and multi-generational problems of bad parenting. We can only pass on to our offspring what we know, and have, for ourselves. People generally do the best they can with what they have; and only the small minority are deliberately cruel and negligent towards children.

The way a child is handled, spoken to, soothed and cared for, all significantly affect the child's developing brain. Clearly, a parent's own dysfunctional childhood will get in the way of them being able to adequately do any of these things for their own child. This is why it is so important for the emotional and psychological damage of the past to be cleaned up and removed as far as possible. If parents-to-be were helped to process their own unresolved traumas, abuse, neglect and lack of self-esteem, then they could become better parents. This would then ripple through to the future generations, and bring significant improvements to our society.

Schools can be a place of both positive and negative learning too. We are taught many facts, dates, and rules; but at worst we also learn how to be verbally and emotionally abused by teachers and peers.

There are brain scanning techniques available (called Single Photon Emission Computerised Tomography, or SPECT scans) that can show which areas of the brain are underdeveloped, underworking or damaged. If children's brains were routinely scanned, say at birth and then again at aged three years, six years and 13 years of age; then treatment protocols could be implemented to correct many such deficits and give that child a much better start in life. Such protocols would include—vital nutritional supplements to enable the improved development of a better functioning brain; adequate and appropriate stimulation; and the vitally important emotional attachment to a reliable and consistent parental figure.

The ways in which we think, feel, eat and drink, and take care of our bodies, all affect the expression of our unique set of genes. We know this from the pioneering work of Dr Bruce Lipton who has shown that your genetic system is not fixed, and that you can change the ways in which your genes are expressed by how you live your life.

(This is called Epi-Genetics) The good news being that it's never too late to make significant changes that will enhance your health, emotional and psychological life as well as your longevity!

So, what does good parenting look and feel like? Well, it comprises of:

> **Emotional bonding with your child.**
>
> **Being attuned to the needs of your child—even before they are expressed.**
>
> **Mirroring the infant's behaviour by using the associated facial expressions and verbal sounds.**
>
> **Being someone the child can 'idealise' and wants to emulate as they grow older.**
>
> **Having a secure attachment to the child, who in turn feels securely attached to you.**
>
> **Assisting the child to develop a positive self-concept, sense of competency and robust self-esteem.**
>
> **Encouraging positive relational skills.**
>
> **Modelling good emotional self-regulation.**
>
> The child is then able to grow up to become a good-enough parent themselves in the future.

In an ideal world every child would be '**WAVED AT**'.....

> **W**anted by their parents and family
>
> **A**ccepted for who they are, and their uniqueness
>
> **V**alued and treasured as the perfect gift that they are
>
> **E**ncouraged to be all they can be
>
> **D**isciplined—with fairness, compassion and empathy

Attuned to—and their basic needs for love, boundaries, and guidance met

Time-worthy—parents spending time talking with, and reading to, their child(ren)—and having fun!

Having a child can be a great healer, as well as a remarkable gift. When society finally realises this and emphasises good-enough parenting then I'm sure we will really see the differences we all want to see in society in general. This would bring enormous financial savings in the longer term too.

It's never too late to 'fill in the gaps' and make up for the deficits in our emotional and psychological education.

Better parents create better members of both the next generation and of the whole of society!

Who Do You Think You Are?

You may think 'I know who I am' .....but I'm sure there are times when you think, feel and react in ways that you neither recognise, or want.

Of course we all have our own unique genetic differences—and our pre-dispositions to certain character traits, our own preferences, our self-concept, and our degrees of introversion and extroversion. Our brains aren't mature until the age of 25 and they also have the ongoing capacity to change as needed in response to our experiences and the meaning we give to these experiences. Our values, beliefs and needs change too—we are not a 'constant' and fixed entity—and that's even before we go down to the Quantum level at which we are mainly empty space anyway!

We also have the added complexity of having a whole 'cast of characters' or 'Sub-Personalities' within us. These came into being as a result of our earlier experiences—particularly traumatic ones—and the people who have influenced us, and the sense we made of these experiences at that time.

The 'decisions', about how to cope and survive your life, were made outside of your awareness and by your immature brain, and they have shaped your present-day life—usually not for the better! Any one of these 'characters' can 'jump into the driving seat' of your life at the most inappropriate and unhelpful moments. This is different from Multiple Personality Disorder—also called Dissociative Identity Disorder,—or Schizophrenia, which are much more profound mental disorders that require specialist psychotherapeutic help.

Perhaps your 'Inner Critic' and/or 'Inner Saboteur' keep making life difficult for you, by constantly nagging at you, and ensuring that you don't succeed in what you set out to do, or to reach your full potential. There may be a Seducer, or a Tragic Victim, or an Aggressive Adolescent lurking inside you—waiting in the wings to jump on stage and take over the show. Maybe your 'People Pleaser' sub-personality wears a very convincing mask—and although you know it's only a mask, and not the 'real' you, you also realise that people only seem to like you when you're wearing it, and so you dare not even try to take it off, and it then becomes a regular feature which shapes your interactions with other people.

Some people are so accustomed to wearing these masks, and living out the sub-personality's role that they have forgotten who they are underneath, and live their lives *as if* the masks were real. They may then in time have a form of 'breakdown', or rather a 'breakthrough', when the real and authentic 'self' breaks through the fake personae and cries out to be seen and acknowledged, desperately trying to get their need for love, understanding and belonging met.

Although we appear 'whole' we are in fact more like a mosaic of different parts which give us the 'illusion' of being solid, stable and predictable. Some people are more cohesive and resilient to life's pressures than others. Not surprisingly, our early experiences, and the meaning we ascribed to them, will have determined how 'well-glued-together' we are.

Without insight into who we now are, and how we became that way; we are condemned to repeat old unhelpful patterns. We may have a conscious hope of changing the outcome of our familiar dramas—but we are doomed to keep repeating these until such time as we introduce knowledge, understanding, and the skills to make the changes we want. We may have to change the subconscious 'Script' of our life and create a new healthier and positive drama, and attract a new cast of people into it too.

Isn't it time you got to know more about the cast of characters in your ongoing play; the roles they play out, and why they do so? You can start by noticing your different sub-personalities when they next appear.

What were the circumstances that triggered their appearance?

How did they take over and change the scene at the time?

When did they then recede into the background again?

Write these things down for each one you encounter. Others will no doubt appear later on when they pick up their particular cue from the wings of the stage. Be aware of this and wait with curiosity and empathy for the role they believe they still need to play out in your life. How can these roles now be updated and revised, or even deleted, from within your life-play altogether?

Knowing about and being able to 'direct' your cast will have significant and positive effects upon your choice of partner, the health of your relationships, how you parent your own children, and how well you succeed in your chosen job or career. In fact, in all areas of your ongoing life-play.

Are You Attached?

To whom or what are you emotionally attached? And how deeply?

Do your attachments enrich your life?

Do you yearn to be able to form, and to keep, meaningful and lasting attachments/ relationships?

Perhaps you avoid attaching to anything or anyone, in the hope of avoiding the pain of inevitable loss—but you then lose the chance of loving, and of being loved by, another; and the feeling of caring for, and receiving the care of, someone special to you; and the profound human need for a sense of 'belonging' with someone whom you value.

Some people become attached to pets or objects as a substitute for the deeper human loving attachment that eludes them, or that they have given up on. The way we are treated as children—predominantly in the first three years—sets up our 'attachment style' and this determines how we subsequently relate to other people in our lives.

In childhood we may have developed different attachment styles with different care-givers—for example if we have been 'looked after' by the Local Authority Care System, or by a mixture of different foster-carers, nannies or relatives. It is only when these experiences and mixed attachment styles become chaotic and disorganised that there is cause for concern and perhaps a need for psychotherapeutic help.

Our early predominant attachment style will be activated by our fear—and can therefore surface at any time. Our brains change due to the attachments we make to other people. We are all 'wired-up' differently depending upon our early childhood experiences of attachment to our 'care-givers'.

In our relationships we can experience difficulties due to the differing attachment styles of ourselves and our partner. These different styles may well be attractive to us initially, but then they can become a problem. For instance one person may want regular contact with their loving family and lots of physical intimacy; and the other person may be more insular, and not feel comfortable with family gatherings and intimacy—either emotional or physical. Don't be fooled into thinking that a long-term relationship is an indicator of a securely attached and compatible couple! Some people 'hide' in a relationship in order to get their needs met, and yet they never really emotionally attach to their partner.

There are significant links between our style of attachment and how we experience loss. The greater the level of emotional attachment the greater the sense of loss—hence not all divorces or deaths bring sorrow or despair—some bring relief, and some bring indifference.

THERE ARE 4 MAIN ATTACHMENT STYLES;

Secure—a fortunate 45% of the overall population are in this category; but this figure varies within different socio-economic groups. It is relatively easy for such people to be emotionally close to others with no concern about being alone. They can confidently ask for help, are more friendly and popular, and have the ability to soothe their own emotional state.

Insecure-Avoidant—about 20% of people. Emotions are shut down and emotional closeness is not trusted, and is therefore avoided. They tend to be insular, independent and self-sufficient; and to expect conflict and rejection. They feel disliked and unworthy of love, and show a lack of sexual intimacy.

Insecure—Ambivalent—about 20% of people. They want/demand attention and then reject it. They do not expect their needs to be met or to have any consistency in their lives. They takes on 'roles' or wear 'masks' to try to gain the approval of others. They can become preoccupied with the fear of loss of another person, and become very clingy, needy and possessive; but then switch to indifference and rejection towards the person.

Disorganised—about 15% of people; again more prevalent in certain socio-economic groups and those whose parent had mental health problems. They show chaotic and unpredictable ways of relating. There is high drama, and a dread of abandonment. Lots of game-playing and manipulation, and a likelihood of co-dependency—which is the needing to be a part in someone else's problematic drama, and of playing out the 'dutiful fixer' or the 'long-suffering martyr' roles. People with this type of attachment deficiency can also be clingy and very fearful of loss or rejection. They have difficulty with appropriate boundaries. They are not usually physically or sexually intimate, although they may be promiscuous. They may seek out Avoidant people with whom to play out their drama of being unloved; or they might find a 'parent' substitute with whom to have an entangled and dysfunctional relationship.

We cannot live without our attachments and we will find anything to attach to rather than have nothing and no-one. A child will even attach to an abusive parent rather than suffer the agony of emotional isolation and abandonment—a physical pain is preferable to a deeply wounding emotional one.

Conventional couple/marital therapy focusses upon intimacy and desire—which is clearly not a suitable focus for the many people who have an insecure attachment style because intimacy requires trust, and this cannot be gained by simply changing their behaviours towards their partner. Instead they first need to work with a competent psychotherapist on their own attachment style difficulties which are blocking their ability to feel and show genuine emotional and physical intimacy towards their partner or spouse.

So, perhaps it's time for you to take a look at your own attachment style, and the quality of your own attachments, and the ways in which these have shaped your relationship successes and failures. The good news is that we can 'learn and earn' a more secure attachment style later in life—if the right conditions exist. It's never too late!

Are You Well-Developed?

From the many studies of the various cultures and sub-cultures that exist in the world, we can see differing developmental levels of the people within any given society or nation, and also how they differ from other cultures and nations. We have all evolved over time from lower and more primitive levels of human development. We all live within our own cultural and societal spectrum and we know our place in it. No level is better or worse than another, it is just at a different stage of development, and so there is never a justification for the ignorance and arrogance of racism, discrimination, ethnic cleansing, oppression or colonialism.

Ken Wilbur, as well as others researchers and authors, has written about 'Spiral Dynamics'—which is the name given to such a study of the different levels of societal development, called 'Memes'. These levels, or memes, are each ascribed their own colour, which has nothing at all to do with skin colour! This is clear, unbiased and objective research into the different levels of human development, behaviour and self-awareness and the ways in which each level functions. Western European society has its own clearly defined 'levels' of functioning.

Some people are literally struggling to survive, to fight off infection, and to find shelter, food and water. Government agencies, and national charities too, have a stated duty to help people on that base level of existence. We know that this is too often not a priority, and that such help is underfunded and undervalued by those with the power to make such changes to the diminished lives of so many people. When those basic needs are adequately met, we can then see society functioning according to higher levels of needs, beliefs and values. People's interest in, and willingness for, 'growth' and change is determined by their knowledge, insight and even the simple realisation that there is a different way of living their lives.

However, as individuals within a culture and society, we can expand and develop significantly in one lifetime as a result of what we are exposed to in our education, opportunities and travels. Or we may choose to play-safe and 'keep the blinkers on' as we slowly plod along on a familiar path. We all have certain choices—the greatest ones being how we perceive events and the meaning we give to them. We may prefer to remain ignorant of what lies beyond our known boundaries, or we may choose to embark upon a lifelong quest for knowledge and personal and spiritual growth. It all depends upon individual circumstances, preferences and opportunities. No-one would expect the starving and homeless of the world to even consider an intellectual, philosophical or spiritual quest—although it's certainly not unheard of. Some people who exhibit the greatest 'power' are those who teach us about love and spiritual values, despite their own meagre lives, struggles and hardships.

Our level of personal self-awareness and development is not fixed—we can rise up and we can slip down on a scale. We may show more development in one area of our lives than another, with different people, situations, influences and environments. We can also see different levels of awareness in the behaviours, perception, and outlook of the members of our own sibling group. Just belonging to the same family as our brothers and sisters does not automatically mean that we will function at the same level as they do even though we may have been exposed to similar experiences during childhood.

The thread that unites everyone is a desire to be happy. We are all doing the best we know how to. We all want to feel good—we just go about that in different ways. From substance abuse and self-harm which alter our mood and emotional state; to criminal behaviour to get us what we want; right through to the joy of giving and acts of kindness to those we know; or life-changing humanitarian work for the good of society or even of mankind.

Our level of development has a profound effect upon our relationships too. We may have made 'marital vows' with someone many years earlier only to have 'grown' away from them and left them behind emotionally, psychologically and spiritually. Relationships may be doomed to fail if they are with someone from a significantly different level to ourself. One partner will have different basic needs to the other, and this can result in frustration and conflict—unless the more 'evolved' partner consciously lives with a compromise, and finds a way to have their spiritual, intellectual and perhaps deeper emotional needs met elsewhere. Perhaps we believe that we can 'take on a project' by educating or supporting a partner/spouse; or that we will be 'the one who can fix him/her'. We can pour our efforts and energy into trying to help someone else to change and 'grow'; but our efforts will most probably be futile, unless that person really wants to improve themselves in some significant way, and they welcome our well-meaning interventions. We should perhaps also realise that any one of us can all too easily be pulled into someone else's 'life-drama' and neglect our own personal needs and development. A life of sacrifice and service to the needs of someone else may seem 'righteous', but does it help you to reach your own full potential in this lifetime? No one changes unless they want to, knows how to, and they can see the personal rewards of changing. We may see the potential in another, but unless they see it themselves and want to walk alongside us we may end up going in different directions. With repeated conflict in a relationship between people at different levels of development, the 'inter-personal bridge' between them becomes damaged and weaker with each argument—until one day there just aren't enough raw materials left behind to rebuild a strong enough bridge for them to meet upon.

It is clear that we do all exist on a continuum and that we 'resonate' best with those who are at a similar place to us. This has an impact upon our choice of friends and partners as well as the interests we pursue, the career we choose, what we choose to read, and other aspects of our daily lives.

We can all raise the level at which we function—if we are aware of the alternatives. We can consciously choose to keep our energy—or vibrational frequency—higher, and to steer ourselves away from the heavier, dense and lower levels which include shame, guilt, fear, jealousy, envy, hatred, aggression, spite, revenge, resentment and pride. The lower levels of functioning also have their own negative attitudes and behaviours, which do not affirm or enhance our lives. Fortunately, we are not condemned to remain at any of the lower levels, even though we may have been culturally conditioned to stay there.

If you want to become more 'developed' as a person then it is up to you to choose to pursue this, assuming that you realise that you do have such a choice!

How Aware Are You?

What does this well-used term 'awareness' actually mean? There are probably many definitions available, but I think the word reflects the extent to which we know about our own level of personal development, of who we are, and what we are experiencing—in our bodies, our thoughts and our emotions—and how we can continue to learn, change and grow.

Aspects of self-awareness include the way in which you look after your body; the ways in which you process and express your emotions; the clarity and relevance of your thoughts and words; your ability to give and receive love; and your openness to higher values and a more spiritually inclined way of life.

We all share the need for sleep, shelter, nourishment and care. Beyond that we need money to bring us wider and greater choices in life and thereby to reduce our levels of stress. How we spend that money, and the choices we make, depend upon our level of 'personal development and awareness'. The level at which you live determines the company you keep, what you read and listen to, and what your hopes and dreams are—whether purely selfish of more selfless. In brief these can be split into three sections although they are not clearly separated and for some people there is an area of overlap with the next stage—i.e. stage 1 to stage 2; and stage 2 to stage 3.

I have given these stages the titles of **_Dormant Awareness, Emerging Awareness and Expanding Awareness_**.

Dormant/Latent Awareness

Awareness here is limited to the Ego and to immediate needs being met. There is a lack of empathy and compassion for others, and a tendency to bigotry, oppression, abuse and violence—even to children and animals. Other people are objectified and 'used' for what they can give—that may be a sense of security, for sex, or to meet the physical needs of a more comfortable life. These people often show a lack of personal health care; they are highly emotional, and their moods may be altered by the use of substances and risky activities. They might have high levels of fear, guilt, shame, blame and jealousy. They are likely to read gossip-based magazines and sensationalistic newspapers, and to watch shame-inducing voyeuristic T.V. 'chat-shows', pornography and violent/horror films. Such people want and expect instant gratification and can be prone to addictions. They often need to belong to a tribe, gang or sports-supporters clan, and to 'wear the colours' to show this allegiance. Their awareness may be increased by such experiences as becoming a parent, serious illness, being a victim of a violent assault, grief and loss, a ghost-sighting, use of clairvoyants, counselling, or perhaps a chance meeting or film that enables insight into a different level of living and being.

EMERGING AWARENESS

There is here less focus on one's own needs being met and this person is becoming more aware of the 'bigger picture'. These people may still be focussed on body 'image,' and needing to wear particular clothing to 'belong' to a group/tribe/clan/gang, or to ease their underlying self-doubts. They may be materialistic—whether it can be afforded or not. They are noticing their emotionality and are finding ways to understand and regulate it. They are becoming aware of broader thinking and reasoning; developing reasoned opinions and clearer, calmer expression. They now seek 'meaning' and 'purpose' in life. They show better self-care and attention to their diet and health, and they are trying to resolve any addictions. They are developing more empathy and consideration of others' needs and perspectives; and they are learning to become more tolerant and accepting of those at the lower level of awareness/development. For these people, there is a greater capacity for forgiveness; love is becoming real, and less conditional upon either their needs being met, or their fears being soothed by someone else. They may read self-help books, and personally relevant articles and stories; and they want to read magazines and newspapers that stimulate balanced and non-political thinking. Counselling, psychotherapy and Psycho-Emotional-Education can assist their insight and awareness.

EXPANDING AWARENESS

Here we find heightened insight, compassion and empathy for others, and an understanding of the stages of the 'Soul Journey' we are all undertaking. People at this level have the ability to see the 'much bigger picture' which includes the Quantum Sciences and the interconnectedness of everything and everyone. They seek like-minded souls who share their higher values, and they know that we all create our own 'reality', and that our thoughts are like tangible matter which attract to us that which we focus upon. They are developing views and aims concerning world peace and coherence, and they work for the good of others—which further enhances their own self and soul development.

Psycho-Emotional-Education and Transpersonal Psychotherapy can help to fill in any gaps to personal and spiritual growth for this more evolved group of people

It is important to reiterate that we are all living our lives at a particular stage of development and we all have our own level of awareness, or lack of it too. We are all doing the best we can with what we've got.

For some people there may be significant comforts and conditions attached to remaining at the dormant levels, and growth and change might not be an option or a desire. The important thing is to remain, as best we can, tolerant and patient towards others with a different perspective, different needs, and different behaviours to ours—even when their views and behaviours adversely impact upon us.

CAN YOU CONFIDENTLY HANDLE DIFFICULT PEOPLE?

These people are everywhere! Sometimes we can simply avoid them but this isn't possible in the family or workplace. Difficult people come in many guises, and they will be someone with whom you, and perhaps others, feel ill-at-ease, emotionally uncomfortable and off-balance.

Maybe you have become the 'difficult' person to be around? Perhaps your own genes and life experiences have meant that you have a tendency to shyness, over-cautiousness, people-pleasing, or a lack of self-esteem/worth. Some people express their self-doubts and sense of inferiority by adopting a 'miserable victim' persona; or they may over-compensate by becoming an 'aggressive bully'. Either can negatively affect everyone around them...this way of 'infecting' others is called Emotional Contagion.

Difficult people are either 'too much or too little' for you. They seem 'too tight or too loose', 'too heavy or too light' and they encroach upon your personal boundaries one way or another. By 'too much/tight/heavy', I mean someone who has a superior attitude, perhaps being narcissistic, and who takes advantage of you, or doesn't show you respect, courtesy or consideration—such as the insensitive critic, or the demanding, condescending, sarcastic or autocratic boss. Or they may attempt to confuse and belittle you with their highly developed intellect and eloquence, losing you in a sea of unfamiliar words and jargon. They may show up as a martyr—always controlling and cleverly turning things around so that they look good, and you don't! They have the belief that others are inferior to themselves, and they expect to dominate or frighten people into doing as they demand. Those who are 'too little/loose/light' seem not fully-present. These people may irritate and/or confuse you when they speak in their vague or meandering way—perhaps in their quest to say something perfectly without causing any distress (due to their fear of being disliked and rejected). These folks might be the simpering employee who acts like a willing and obedient slave; or they may be someone who tries to manipulate you into meeting their insatiable needs by using the tools of 'guilt' or 'duty'. They might present themselves to you as airy-fairy, helpless and scatterbrained, perhaps abdicating responsibility for themselves and their choices by happily passing every aspect of their lives over to 'the Universe' to solve for them. They may be the sycophantic, syrupy, sugar-sweet people-pleaser who you find it hard to challenge lest you be seen as cruel and nasty!

I speak here as a difficult person myself, albeit in certain circumstances. In my case I can almost immediately switch into becoming superior and rude if I am being lied to, or ignored, by sales or customer services staff; or if my integrity is challenged and I am wrongly suspected or accused of making a mistake, or of being in the wrong, (assuming that this isn't the case of course!); or if my progress is thwarted in some way—even, on a bad day, by someone who is walking too slowly in front of me and blocking my way on the pavement, or if a check-out queue is moving too slowly due to incompetent staff or a time-wasting customer ahead of me. I'm at my worst—as my daughter will attest to—if I'm spoken to in a patronising or condescending way by a shop worker, who is after all only doing what they've been trained to do....be false and pretend that they genuinely care about, or are interested in, the customer/client. Even writing about such incidents is beginning to annoy me.... deep breaths.....be calm....tranquil and serene Maxine! I have therefore had cause to wonder how I would advise someone to handle such a difficult person. It would need some understanding of the possible reasons for the difficult behaviour, as well as learning how to calm and regulate our own emotional response to the difficult person, and any necessary confidence-building skills.

If you follow the recently published 'advice' of a celebrity hypnotist who offers to 'make you confident' you will just imagine a 'confident you' ahead of you and then 'walk' into this person—several times; and then tap various points on your body too. However these Neuro-Linguistic Programming and Emotional Freedom Techniques will still not give you the skills needed in the real world to enable you to cope with the intense anxiety that a lack of confidence brings when you are faced with a real challenge from a difficult person or situation.

In brief, there are 3 stages to consider: the event/or anticipated event; your inner dialogue and belief system; and the way you then choose to behave. We cannot change an event but we can change our perception of it, as well as how we talk to and soothe ourselves.

Furthermore, we can learn ways of speaking and expressing ourselves that are both confident and assertive.

Unassertive behaviour is either passive—whereby you just agree to give-in to the needs, wants and preferences of the other person in order to please them and to avoid any conflict; or it is aggressive—when you try to dominate and control the other person. However, assertive behaviour is neither of these extremes, and instead it comes from a place of 'I have the right to say what I experience and what I want/prefer/need and to share this with you'. This way of expression is therefore confident, rational and matter-of-fact. It asserts our own position without any expectations of how the other person will feel or behave as a result of our disclosure. There is no right or wrong. It just is as it is. A disclosing and sharing of our inner world with another, but only to the extent with which we feel comfortable.

There are several reasons why we may find it difficult to assert ourselves in a confident manner. We were probably not taught at school how to be confident and assertive—quite the opposite in most cases I'm sure! For many of us, these skills would not have been welcomed back at home, and so we have had to wait much later to even know that there was a different way to deal with difficult people and situations. We may have had parents who were not themselves clear, calm and emotionally-balanced, and so they couldn't then model self-respect and good self-esteem to us. Perhaps as children we were not invited to talk about ourselves and our opinions or perceptions. We may not have felt of value or worth in the most important place—our homes. We may have been bullied at home, at school or at work and we can now unknowingly 'invite' people to treat us badly because that is what we know, and expect. Under pressure we may still operate like the wounded-child we once were, and have only the limited verbal expression of this young inner-child. When we are anxious we cannot think clearly and we cannot express ourselves clearly. Instead we are predominantly focussed in our Emotional or Limbic brain—ready to fight/flee/freeze or flop. None of these experiences will have helped us to be well-grounded, confident and assertive adults.

The good news is that we can all learn to develop a new 'inner dialogue' that supports and affirms us and our right to be treated well by others—as well as the right to walk away from people who aren't able to treat us well. Learning and understanding about ourselves is the first step to change. We can learn what our healthy 'boundaries' are and how to set and maintain them in the face of opposition and conflict. We also need to learn about how and why we experience difficulties with others; and which part of this is our responsibility and which part isn't. We can develop skills that will enable us to express ourselves clearly and effectively.....and to handle those 'difficult people' we will inevitably encounter. There are also several levels of communication to learn about—ranging from the level of shallow chit-chat to the most personal self-disclosures; and there are different ways or styles of communicating effectively too. This can be like learning a whole new language and a new way of communicating with people from all walks of life—which really is liberating and empowering, both personally and professionally.

If we can see beneath the behaviour to the wounded child who resides within the difficult person, it helps us to acknowledge their pain and their need to present themselves as they do. From this place of empathy and compassion we can then see that they are doing their best in a situation that they are trying to control—they are just going about it all wrong by being too much or too little—the top-dog or the under-dog. If we can also learn to understand how our own history may have shaped how we react to challenges—whether these be aggressive and threatening, or perhaps needy, or baffling, or guilt-inducing—we can reassure ourselves that as adults in the present day we can keep ourselves calm and safe in the face of such difficulties, and retain our competent adult perspective and use a new vocabulary which asserts our rights, needs, wants and preferences.

Mental Health—How Crazy are You?

We are all crazy—in someone else's eyes, and judgement!

We tend to think of mental illness as a description of profound psychiatric problems with a specific diagnosis, as categorized in the Diagnostic and Statistical Manual of the American Psychiatric Association. (The latest and 5th issue has recently been drafted and has already caused controversy because of the medicalisation of many behaviours previously considered to just be a part of life's natural cycle, such as teenage angst.) These diagnoses usually have a corresponding pharmaceutical drug, or cocktail of drugs, as 'treatment'—although other methods such as Electro-Convulsive-Therapy do still exist, despite a lack of evidence as to its efficacy! We have come a long way from the bedlam or asylum days of the past and yet mental illness is still rife in every society.

Lack of basic needs such as adequate nutrition, care, shelter and education; and prolonged drug and alcohol use; and exposure to violent traumas, all exacerbate the onset and ongoing state of mental illness. Sadly these factors are common everyday experiences for a large and neglected sector of our society. The behaviours of such people, with deficits in their brain's functioning capacity, has far-reaching consequences. Babies are born to parents whose brains are not fully functioning and this is passed on to the baby—along with inadequate nutrition to enable the baby's brain to develop properly. Damaged children become damaged adults who find other damaged adults, and they pass on their damage to their offspring...and the cycle continues.

News reports here in Britain have spoken of the intentional torture and murder of children by relatives who believed them to be witches and 'possessed by evil spirits'. This seems crazy to most of us, and yet is a prevailing belief in parts of Africa. Cultural differences bring with them beliefs and behaviours that other cultures judge to be 'crazy'. We can easily become de-sensitized to much of what we hear about in the world, because we simply cannot absorb it all and we feel powerless to do anything to prevent such crazy things from happening. We live in a crazy world, where, surely all of the following could be deemed by someone to be insane/crazy:

Racism—and discrimination, oppression and violence against another person, simply because their ancestors originated from a different continent. According to the experts, we all originated from East Africa anyway!

Homophobia—and violence against a person who has different sexual preferences and needs.

Fundamentalist religions—whose followers threaten death to those who do not follow their particular code of behaviour and societal norms; or to those they deem as having insulted a prophet or leader.

Cultural norms—such as the stoning of women accused of adultery, the chopping off of a thief's hand, honour killing, and arranged marriages.

Slavery—the domination of, and cruelty towards, another human being.

Human trafficking and exploitation

Female circumcision forced upon young girls

Preventable diseases and poverty—whilst wealth exists elsewhere in the country.

Corporate greed—and the psychopathic personality traits of the few who control the flow of wealth in Western society.

Cruelty to children—particularly in the 'feral underclass', as it has been described in the media; children taught to cage-fight with one another for the 'entertainment' of the so-called adult spectators.

Paedophilia—and the grooming and sexual exploitation of, and violence towards children.

Foreign aid—sent to countries with already enough wealth of their own for 'space programs', or for weapons designed and intended for war.

Destruction of much of the planet—fuelled by selfishness, greed, ignorance and arrogance.

Cruelty to animals—dog-fighting, badger baiting, fox-hunting; and 'festivals' where animals are sacrificed for 'pleasure/fun'.

Gender selection—the killing of newborns because they are the 'wrong' gender.

Huge Government waste—Unnecessary Quangos, consultants, independent reports/enquiries; moth-balled projects, and outright fraud.

Prohibition of contraceptives—by certain religious 'leaders' despite the prevalence of AIDS, HIV, sexually transmitted diseases and unwanted pregnancies.

Space travel—whilst people are starving and without basic medical care.

Excessive Legislation—such as Health and Safety rulings which have resulted in death (the recent media reports regarding emergency services being unwilling, due to the prevailing Health and Safety rules, to rescue a person who drowned in a few inches of water.)

Cyber-bullying—the threatening and offensive treatment of people via the internet and social media sites in particular.

These all show a lack of empathy, compassion, care or concern for the health, safety or well-being of others. In some of the examples above, there is also a 'projection' of badness onto a 'victim', be that an individual, group, class, or culture/society. This projection is then used as a form of justification for, and a normalising of, crazy and cruel behaviours. This is accompanied by a ruthless selfishness that says—"I matter more than you, I have the right to use and damage/destroy you."

Having worked as a psychotherapist with some individuals who have committed assaults, and even murder; and having all too often heard of intense cruelty having been inflicted upon a vulnerable child, I wonder why we don't scan the brains of the perpetrators and find out 'why' they do what they do—and then give them the effective treatment, wherever it is possible, for those areas of the brain that are just not working properly. If we could neurologically determine the causes of the lack/loss of self-control, or identify an actual mental illness, we could then focus upon effective remedies and preventions which would in turn save the pain and devastation of so many innocent victims and their families. Most people exhibit neuroses of some sort, as well as mild 'personality disorder' traits. These may go unnoticed in the crazy world that we all inhabit.

So, what does good, robust mental health look like?

I think it involves:

Emotional stability and self-regulation.

Rational thinking, and an ability to control and disarm any irrational thoughts.

A positive self-esteem and body image.

The ability to withstand challenges and criticism.

Not allowing the past to negatively affect the present or future, and therapeutically healing the past.

Showing genuine care and compassion towards children, animals and the vulnerable in society.

Having a sense of empathy and sympathy towards others.

Not obediently going along with the crowd/mob/tribe—but of finding your own positive pathway.

Congruence—what is felt on the inside is portrayed sensitively and assertively on the outside.

Authenticity—being 'real' and genuine, and only wearing a 'mask' if you consciously choose to, for a short time, and for a specific and valid purpose.

Let us not forget that our brains are not fully developed until we are about 25 years of age—and that they then have what is called 'plasticity' which allows the brain to change, and to increase its neuronal connections and pathways, in response to our physical and emotional needs and experiences. It's never too late to learn a better way of relating to yourself and to others. Then a crazy world becomes a little less crazy each time someone takes responsibility for, and finds the right path towards, healing their own psychological and emotional wounds.

Do You Feel Ashamed of Yourself?

We often use the word 'shame' to represent the words 'unfortunate' or 'disappointing', as in the phrase "that's a shame" or "what a shame."

In fact 'shame' is a very powerful emotion—it has been referred to by leading psychotherapists as 'the master emotion' because of the huge impact it has upon us. Shame can be experienced by an individual, a family, a culture, or even by a nation (ethnic cleansing, holocaust, colonialism, slavery etc.). Shame is associated with the lowest levels of energy—it actually robs us of our energy. Contrast this with happiness, joy and bliss which raise our energy levels up high.

We must be clear to separate shame from guilt. Guilt is an appropriate emotion of remorse when we have done something that we know to be wrong;, and which has in some way hurt another person either physically or emotionally. We feel guilty and we can then choose whether to put things right, or not. Some people try to induce guilt in others—the 'guilt trip'—as a way of manipulating them to get their own needs met by that other person. If this often happened to us when we were small we probably learned to feel bad each time, and to then change our behaviour to please the other person—but at a cost to our own authenticity.

On the other hand shame is associated with believing **yourself to be bad**—it is not badness associated with an act, but with your sense of yourself, of who you are at your core. No-one is born feeling shame—it is passed on through the generations of our family (intergenerational shame), as well as being picked up from our other caregivers, teachers, religious institution, military training and many other sources. We use shame to control and squash people. When people feel shame they feel low, depleted and worthless, and they can easily be manipulated, oppressed and exploited.

To feel shame is to have reached the end of a spectrum of emotions, which includes embarrassment and self-consciousness. Of course shame is much greater than these other levels, which all still involve our focussing upon ourselves and judging ourselves as not-OK, not good-enough, a failure, and not worthy to be around. When in 'shame' we feel exposed to the world, raw, extremely vulnerable, loathsome, and we want to hide—literally, or by wishing that the ground could just open up and swallow us. We look downwards or away from others, we hide our face and we shrink our body size as we slump into the pit of shame.

Most families (about 90%) can be described as 'dysfunctional' to some degree, and many use shame as a weapon to gain power over other members of the group/family/tribe. We also see 'counter-shame' when there is an exchange of shaming, blaming and demeaning comments between people which are designed and intended to make the other person feel even worse. We may disguise this as 'harmless and playful banter' but the look in the eyes of the person on the receiving end of this, shows that it is far from being either harmless or fun. If we have been chronically shamed we can continue to 'feel bad' for most of our waking lives; and even sub-consciously seek partners and situations which repeat the shame-inducing emotions is us. We can become addicted to feeling the intensity of shame. Some people have sub-consciously made a link between the 'peak experience' of shame and sexual arousal, resulting in psycho-sexual, relationship and intimacy problems.

As shame is such a debilitating and common emotion it makes sense that we try to defend ourselves against its impact. As well as firing out counter-shaming comments, we may also use comments that 'limit the impact' of what someone else is saying or doing to us. We try to give the impression of not caring about it; or we might become detached and not accept kindness or help from anyone, in case we might be seen as vulnerable or receiving 'charity'.

A 'shame-based' person may present themselves to the world as very proud and boastful, or perhaps as being self-righteous—as a defence against their true feelings of shame and vulnerability. But if we imagine the wounded-child behind this attempt at ego-inflation we can have some compassion for their struggle to convince themselves and others that they really are OK. We can also see aggression as a defence, in the face of the threat of shame. When a vulnerable person perceives a shame-inducing comment (particularly if that person comes from a background of abuse or neglect), they can react with the pent-up rage that has been stored up from earlier shame-inducing episodes in their life. They can lash out uncontrollably; often with very serious or even fatal results for their victim—particularly if alcohol is involved as this loosens the inhibitors that usually keep such rage hidden deeper in the psyche. Bad parenting affects not only the children, but the society these children then live in as they grow older.

Suicide can be an extreme way for some people to avoid the public judgement and shame they anticipate, and dread, will result from the exposure both of their act(s) of wrong-doing, and of their defective character, which has now been shown to be weaker than had been previously portrayed. Such is the power of shame to disintegrate the sense of our worth and our right to belong in society.

People often lie to hide their shame—only to feel more shame when such lies are exposed. These are not the compulsive lies of the personality-disordered person, who may create a whole fictitious life with a complex web of lies. Such disordered people tend to be devoid of shame, remorse, empathy, consideration or care for another person's well-being and feelings.

We also see the inflated ego of the 'Narcissist' who attempts to appear in every way better than other people. Their facade can be hard to challenge—particularly in psychotherapy when they will project badness onto the therapist. Despite having to engage only the 'best' and most expensive and renowned therapist—as becomes their own (perceived) elevated status. They will most probably end the therapy very soon; and thereby ensure that they retain the 'power' of being the one to reject the other person. Genuine empathy can be a way 'under the radar' when attempting to reach the real feelings of shame of the Narcissist—but only if sensitively and genuinely intended, and not just as a weapon to expose their deep underlying vulnerability.

Many of us have dreams in which we are exposed—perhaps naked—and we feel the force of shame; and the relief of waking up from it too. Our dreams are a way of processing our emotions and unresolved thoughts and ideas of the day. These 'shame' dreams do not represent a fantasy we necessarily wish to act out in our waking state!

Shame was unavoidable when we were children, and it was used to control us; but as adults we must get a grip on shame, shine a light on it and take away its power to sap our energy and well-being. We have a choice about whether we allow others to induce shame in us with their words or actions. We can instead learn to be brave and to stand up for the wounded child inside us who didn't have a voice back then and who needs you to now rise to their defence and not allow anyone else to diminish you with shame. When shame is exposed, disarmed and rejected not only does it disintegrate but it shows us that it is after all an expression of the weakness in the one using it to manipulate and control someone else's feelings. Don't allow it!

SELF-RELIANCE

Self-reliance is an inner state of knowing that you are robust, resilient and resourceful enough to tackle the challenges and difficulties that life will inevitably throw at you. It is formed from the meaning you have given to your own life experiences, which in turn then overlay your innate personality; as well as from what you have seen 'modelled' by the self-reliant people you have had contact with.

With the right circumstances and guidance we can gradually develop those all important characteristic traits of courage, competence, determination, persistence, tenacity and resilience. We must learn not to allow our setbacks, disappointments and failures to reinforce any negative beliefs we still hold from childhood. Instead we should rationally evaluate any negative experiences—free from their emotional components—and see what we can learn from them; and what we might want to change about ourselves to enable us to better handle such challenges in the future. If we find that our plan or strategy was flawed in some way, we can then create effective ways to change it.

It can be hard to overcome our early emotional wounds, but if we can see them as the learning opportunities they are meant to be, we can grow and become more of a robust, realistic and grounded adult, who can 'take care of business' in our life. Our new-found inner strength will then buffer us against future storms, as we accumulate more opportunities to become greater than we were. Otherwise our old 'programming' and 'script' will just keep repeating themselves over and over again, and keep us stuck in the old drama of our lives.

As we become more able to think, plan and take appropriate action for ourselves, we don't need to rely upon a 'life-coach' or 'cognitive-mentor' to do our common-sense functioning for us. With our own 'ego-strength' we can take care of our own needs and carry out our plans, and reach our goals, with persistent effort.

As we develop into a self-reliant adult we can, paradoxically, become a more reliable person for others too. We can also have better relationships, because we are not looking for the other person to validate us or prove their love for us. As we calm and soothe our own emotional state and choose to shift gear into our sensible reasoning and rational adult, we can actually then loosen up to become more playful and intimate. This is because we dissolve the 'neurotic' neediness and game playing that is so common in many relationships.

As a parent we can greatly assist our child's sense of self-reliance—something which they are usually pushing to have from an early age anyway! We can offer them graded challenges and opportunities to learn new skills and talents—which don't have to be expensive. We can support and encourage their emerging sense of self-worth and esteem, by giving appropriate and well-timed praise in an honest and empathic way—without any sarcasm or back-handed compliments, and certainly not by using ridicule or any other form of 'put-down' to the sensitive soul of the child. Negative behaviour should be called just that and separated from the positive goodness of the child itself. Some bad behaviour should simply be ignored—as long as it isn't dangerous to anyone in any way.

Smothering and over-protective parenting, whilst well-meaning, robs a child of the ability to form and adhere to necessary boundaries in their life, or to tackle any challenges head-on. Learning to delay gratification is also important, but it becomes harder in modern times when the media brainwashes us into thinking that to 'be somebody' you must 'have it and have it NOW!' The sense of personal achievement from working towards, and attaining, a goal can be lost by the premature satisfaction of a desire.

As a psychotherapist I have worked with many people who didn't have the chance to develop self-reliance because their early lives were dominated by chaos and fear; and they then had to try to develop a sufficient sense of adult self-reliance at a much later time in their lives, in order to function better in the world.

Other clients had parents whose own narcissism meant that the client grew up with the expectation that they must succeed, perhaps academically or in sports/drama etc. so that their parent(s) could bolster their own fragile self-esteem with the glory of their 'perfect' offspring's achievements. Individual personality development in the child then becomes stifled, as does the ability to rely upon themself and direct the path of their own life.

By contrast, other clients have reported having had a good/great/ideal childhood—which sadly had not prepared them for the trials and tribulations of life. They had insufficient skills with which to regulate their emotions or deal with a later life crisis—such as redundancy, divorce, business failure, being burgled or defrauded etc. and they were completely thrown off balance by circumstances that a more self-reliant and resilient person would be better equipped to deal with.

We live in a 'something for nothing' culture nowadays, which relies upon the goodwill, duty, pity and support of other people or the State. This dependence does not develop an individual's character or enhance their personality. Believing in yourself and your ability to create your own 'Life of Choice' prevents you from enduring a life of dependency or passivity.

* Repeating your positive intentions, with deep and heartfelt feeling, has been proven to bring about positive and tangible results which will strengthen and reinforce your sense of self-reliance.

* It's never too late to learn how to change and to be better than you used to believe you ever could be.

* You are the only one who will never leave you, so you might as well be sure that you can at least rely upon yourself!

Whom Can You Trust?

If only we knew! We can't even fully trust ourselves sometimes. Our sub-conscious minds—which run our lives over 90% of the time—can make us behave in ways that may shock and embarrass us. Therapeutic work may encourage us to develop a more trusting attitude and to take the risk that others won't betray, use or manipulate us—but this may be somewhat naïve.

We cannot tell by appearances who can be trusted and how far, or what the exceptions to that trust might be. It can take many years to build up trust in a friendship or other relationship and many of us have been betrayed by the very people we deeply believed we could trust never to let us down. To be let-down, hurt and disappointed, can reinforce our lack of trust, and we might then extend this to generally mistrusting everyone. This would be an attempted defence against being hurt again, but unfortunately it cannot be guaranteed to work. and it brings with it its own down-sides such as too much self-sufficiency and over-independence, loneliness, and feelings of isolation and disconnection from the vibrant intimacy that life has to offer.

Most of us crave a deep contact, involving genuine emotional and physical intimacy, with someone 'special' to us—someone whom we can 'trust'. However, some people have given up on trying, or hoping, to get those needs met, and have instead settled for an 'entanglement' rather than a full relationship—wherein they may feel a bit safer whilst they get only their basic human needs met—but they will not be truly happy with such a shallow, selfish and fear-based arrangement.

It is probably obvious that our childhood has had a big impact upon our base-line level of trust. This will have been set up before the age of two years—and therefore too early for us to have a verbal memory of this time. If we experienced cold and rigid, or smothering and intrusive parenting, abandonment and/or rejection, abuse, trauma, neglect, or the chaotic behaviours of care-giver(s) due to substance abuse or mental ill-health, then our deeper personal boundaries will have been violated and we will have been powerless to stop that. We would have wanted and needed to rely upon stability, predictability, and loving care, but our parents may not have been able to provide these, even if they had wanted to.

The quality and availability—both physical and emotional—of our care-giver will have affected the way our brain was developing and how safe, secure and trusting we felt; as well as our ability to seek help and comfort from other people, and to emotionally attach to them and form healthy relationships. We had no say in the way things were back then, but as adults we do now have the power to change our 'life-script' and become more trusting of some people—but we must be discerning! It can be potentially life-threatening to put our trust in the wrong people or in the outcome of events.

Fundamentally, we want to be able to trust that those in whom we invest our time and emotions will have integrity. That they will be honest and reliable. That they will not go back on their word. That they will show us consideration and understanding, and, hopefully, empathy and compassion too. We should also perhaps consider whether we offer these things in return, or do we expect it to be a one-way street?

When it comes to sex, money or business then our ability to be trustworthy can be weakened, but it is when these issues are involved that we need the most trust in ourselves and in other people. We cannot 'see' the motives or intentions of others, and yet by having a suspicious attitude which keeps people at bay we may miss out on honest, genuine, caring contact. We have to find out what someone really wants with us. In any interaction or relationship we all want to know 'what's in it for me'?

We are all entitled to honesty and respect from others and instead of holding back—for fear of appearing intrusive and interrogatory—we need to ask clear and specific questions, in a calm and assertive way, and without shying away from any deeper emotional response and disclosure that may follow. We must also be able to cope with any disappointments that another's self-disclosure or behaviour may bring. Depending upon what is asked of us and what type of relationship we want to form, we must take responsibility for finding out as much as we can about the inner world of the other person (or as far as their personal boundaries around self-disclosure will allow.) Finding out about someone's background, their values and ambitions, what they respect in a person, what they find unacceptable, what makes their heart sing, how angry have they been, when and how they behaved (they may not of course tell you the full story) can all help us to 'know' more about the other on a deeper and more important level. We can then decide whether we even want to place our trust in them or not. Their body language will give away important clues too, and our instincts can be a valuable guide here. However, beware of the seasoned salesman and con-man who will have deliberately adjusted their body language so as to trick others for their own ends. There will always be 'leaks' of the truth shown in their body language, or verbal 'slips', but it may take a trained eye and ear to spot these.

Ongoing media 'news' shows us that we cannot trust in an elected Government 'system' to provide basic human needs to the sick and vulnerable. We cannot trust in the efficacy of the Health Service, or that our children will be well educated. We cannot trust the 'money-managers' in our society not to be selfish and greedy. We cannot trust that what we read in the newspapers is the truth. We cannot fully trust in our Police Force and legal system. We cannot even trust that our telephone conversations or e-mails are private!

We have to trust ourselves to be able to cope without having the degree of trust we might prefer to have. We have to trust that we will be able to cope with betrayal and disappointments, with being misled, deceived or exploited, with temporary loss of our hopes and dreams, or loss of a relationship, or loss of money and/or business.

To become a more trusting person, we first have to be committed to wanting and trying to be more trusting, and then to decide who and what is the safest to trust. Later we can then extend this to putting trust in someone or something a little more risky and so on, knowing that we have the inner resources and self-reliance to cope with any unfortunate disappointments without letting them squash our developing ability to trust in the prevailing goodness of life—despite there being a few untrustworthy characters around.

We cannot function without a basic level of trust in the goodness and kindness of at least part of our community. Without such trust the world would be a very threatening and frightening place indeed.

Does Your Fear Imprison You?

The UK media has given us tragic news of a racially-motivated fatal shooting; slaughter of several family members by the partner of one of the deceased; death of well-known people due to ill-health;

and reports about the lack of care for the elderly and vulnerable in society. It can be hard not to be afraid of what is outside our front door, or ahead of us in life, but we must get this powerful emotion into perspective before it dominates our lives.

Fear is regarded as one of the 'lower' emotions and is linked to survival. As cave-dwellers in the distant past, we were right to fear an attack from a sabre-toothed tiger, or other threats to our existence. Our primitive brains haven't really caught up to the present day in some ways and we still react to a real or imagined threat as if it were life threatening. Fear of redundancy and poverty feels similar to us to the fear of being chased down and mauled to death by a hungry predator!

Your brain cannot tell the difference between a real threat and one that is vividly imagined—it reacts in the same way. Our primitive fight/flight/freeze/flop response system is activated, causing the stress hormones of adrenalin and cortisol to flood our bodies—which can harm both our brain and the health of our immune system if it happens repeatedly.

We all have a part of our brain called the Limbic brain, which registers and processes our emotions. The Emotional/Limbic brain—in particular the area called the Amygdala—can be 'over-aroused' by sudden and/or frequent threats, both real and imagined. It then becomes hard to 'turn-down' the arousal in this area, and we see the results of hyper-arousal in both Post-traumatic Stress Disorder and Prolonged-Duration Stress Disorder, whereby we remain 'alert' and 'vigilant' for any potential further threats to our safety, both when awake and asleep.

Our fears, at different levels, are fuelling so much of our lives—from the careers we have chosen; the relationships we have; to our home lifestyles and the levels of our wealth and success.

What do you fear?

Common fears include;-

- loss of love/care/attention/support/safety/security
- humiliation/rejection/abandonment
- being trapped/confined in our life.
- being seen as not 'good enough', or unable to cope, or seen by others as a failure
- having our trust betrayed by another
- loss of 'status' and esteem
- losing our health and/or sanity
- vulnerability and dependency upon others
- physical and/or emotional pain
- isolation and loneliness
- facing our past and its effects upon us
- death, particularly if painful and/or alone.

If we allow it to be so, we can become governed, restrained, and thwarted by our own fears. They hold us down and tie us up so that we cannot feel free, fully alive or spontaneous. Instead we 'play safe' in our lives—and perhaps we then activate some of our other fears instead. It is not surprising that we try very hard to avoid experiencing what we fear, but this avoidance comes at a cost to our authenticity as a person. We lose sight of what we were fully meant to be, and we don't reach our full potential.

Well it's time to loosen the grip of our fears and to become free to take sufficient risks that enable us to have new experiences which affirm who we are and allow us to grow into who we can become. The first steps to this come from learning and understanding about how our past has shaped and moulded our lives in the present day;

and then comes learning how to regulate our emotions and to use our more adult-brain to soothe and calm ourselves, and to see things more realistically. False Evidence Appearing Real is often true! We should at least be able to tell the difference and respond with our calm adult awareness, rather than simply react from a childlike emotional state.

Life will bring to you the very things that you fear anyway—the 'dark night of the soul'—so that you can grow beyond your fears and be free of them. Realising that this is inevitable, and learning how to cope and move on will help you to develop your character and soul for the rest of your journey ahead.

FORGIVE AND FORGET?

There's a commonly used saying 'Forgive and Forget' and yet forgiveness isn't necessarily linked to forgetting, and we can forgive whilst still holding on to the memory, and impact, of that which has been forgiven. We can choose who and what we will, or will not, forgive. Certain events may have had only a minimal impact upon us and our lives, whereas others will have made our lives seem very hard to endure. There is a whole spectrum of 'that which has the potential to be forgiven by you' and there may also be some things you feel incapable of forgiving—and would not be appropriate for you to forgive either. Sometimes an apology is sufficient to wipe the slate clean, provided it is genuine, heartfelt, considerate and well-timed.

A genuine apology has 4 stages;

* Acknowledging, and taking responsibility for, the wrong-doing.
* Giving an honest explanation as to why it happened.
* A sincere and earnest 'sorry'.
* A way of 'putting it right', or atonement, if at all possible.

A slight rejection or rebuff, or genuine mistake which has been properly apologised for, will be easy to forgive—and probably to forget too. Something having more emotional and physical impact upon you, such as having been bullied, slandered, betrayed, humiliated, rejected or abandoned will be harder to forgive.

Further along that scale we have situations where our 'boundaries' have been violated—such as with childhood abuse, rape, assault, fraud, theft and robbery. At the extreme end of the spectrum is murder—in its many forms. The worst crime against us must be the murder of someone we love—particularly of a child. It is incomprehensible to most people to forgive such a terrible act, and yet we do occasionally see news coverage of the parent(s) of a murder victim saying that they forgive the perpetrator. Usually this is linked to the forgiving parent having deep religious beliefs—which may also include the sanctity of life.

We may well have a need for justice, or revenge. Often the legal system fails to provide the justice needed, and revenge can result in further crime and injury. If a large institution, such as the National Health Service, is to blame for our pain and loss, it can be a very lengthy and costly process trying to get the acknowledgement and apology we need. Holding onto hate and resentment can make a life bitter and shrivelled, yet despite this we may still find it impossible to forgive those who are to blame.

We might have compassion for a perpetrator who has had a difficult childhood; but so have many other hundreds of thousands of people who would find it inconceivable to commit a crime. So many of the violent crimes we hear of nowadays involve young people whose brains are not yet mature; whose diet and lifestyle mean that their brains cannot function properly; and whose need for belonging and protection is found in a gang instead of at home.

With such 'mitigating circumstances' as these we can perhaps feel some sympathy and compassion—but that may not be enough to allow us to forgive. We may condemn ourselves to carry the 'hot coals' of hate for the rest of our lives.

What are the limits of your capacity to forgive?

What will you never forgive, and why?

What would have to happen for you to be able to forgive an existing wrong-doing against you?

What have you forgiven yourself for doing?

What guilt are you still holding onto that you cannot forgive yourself for—even if you have been forgiven by another for this?

Perhaps you feel guilty for not being a good enough parent, friend, partner or sibling. Maybe you have done or said something you regret whilst you were under the influence of alcohol or drugs. Holding onto guilt and shame squashes and blocks us. These are heavy emotions to carry around. You owe it to yourself to be courageous enough to make a genuine apology and atonement either in person; or in the case of a deceased person, in the 'unsent-letter/e-mail' form. Just 'externalising' your feelings on paper helps you to process them yourself, and to begin to file them away instead of them holding you down, and holding you back, in many areas of your life. It helps if you can feel genuine compassion for yourself and your own struggles and challenges that have played a part in how you have behaved towards others. We cannot of course change the past but we can change the way it affects our present and future.

Asking for forgiveness can seem like asking for a pardon, a wiping out of the memory of what was done. Saying 'I forgive you' can be shallow and meaningless unless it is backed up with a reason that is truly robust and valid. Being able to understand that the other person didn't know any better and did the best they knew how with the resources they had is some comfort, some of the time.

If there is anything positive about forgiveness it is that we do it for ourselves, and not for the other person.

Are You Lonely—Or Alone?

Being alone doesn't necessarily equate with loneliness. Many people enjoy the calmness and clarity of being alone for relatively long periods of time—rather than being involved in the drama of other people's lives. As Sartre said "Hell is other people." Paradoxically, being amongst people can be a lonely experience, if we don't have a deep and meaningful connection with them.

We all have to wrestle with the awareness of, and the differences between, our basic human needs and our spiritual needs; and how we can get these adequately met, so that we can live a comfortable earthly life which is also spiritually vital, growthful and enriching. We all need to balance our time spent alone in reflection, contemplation and planning; with our time spent with others, sharing ourselves with them at many different levels. Both ways of being can significantly nourish who we are and who we can become.

A sense of loneliness can be something we have become accustomed to from a very early age. Having parents/care-givers who were not emotionally available and attuned to you, or being amongst siblings and family members who were noticeably 'different' from you, induces a sense of semi-isolation. Of being there but not really being there; of 'going through the motions' in our dealings with others. Of being lonely in a crowd. Amongst others, yet still feeling solitary and alone.

Some of us had a less-than-good-enough childhood, and formed few attachments with people because the people around us were neglectful, unreliable or threatening. Instead we may have formed attachments to animals, objects, hobbies, or perhaps to our own ideas, wishes and dreams. To have an 'Attachment Disorder' can condemn us to a life without meaningful and rewarding human relationships. Or instead, as we mature, we can slowly learn to build trust in a stable and reliable person, and to take the risk of making an emotional attachment to them—which carries with it an inherent risk of loss and emotional pain which would of course take time to recover from.

Some people will have a self-imposed aloneness, and perhaps loneliness too, because they have in the past felt 'trapped' in relationships with their family or spouse/partner, and they then avoid getting close to other people, as a way of ensuring they don't feel trapped and thwarted again. The obvious cost of this is to remain without the deeper intimate connection that most people strongly desire.

Internet dating sites and chat rooms offer a relatively quick, easy and inexpensive way to make contact with other people—but they are not a salve for deeper loneliness. Indeed the disappointment and rejection often reported by users of such sites can only add to feelings of alienation and isolation. Don't allow loneliness to push you into bad relationships. You may feel lonely but you can still be discerning about who you want to spend your time with, and how this will enrich your life.

The 'commitment phobic' person may deeply desire loving contact and to have some of their needs met by another; but they cannot take that step to an exclusive, reciprocal and emotionally intimate relationship. This may be because they have only experienced bad relationships, or they may have a core-belief that they don't deserve to be in a good relationship. Or they may have felt 'engulfed' in a previous relationship and lost the sense of their own separate identity; or they may have been over-burdened with responsibilities in their past, and they fear that this will happen again. A partner of such a person may only found this out after years of hoping, waiting, disappointment and broken promises.

Some people ensure that their lives are very busy, and that they are in demand and having a 'full-on life'. This can be just a sham—and an attempt to fully occupy their time so as to distract them from their deeper gnawing sense of loneliness. Distraction activities such as over-working and over-spending can also be attempts to avoid the intense pain of alone-ness. Having lots of superficial 'friends' may help someone to avoid deeper intimacy with anyone in particular, but it can also lead to feeling lonely, despite a broad network of 'contacts'—particularly so in our 'social media' age. One deeper intimate relationship is more beneficial to our soul than a large number of casual acquaintances could ever be.

We all like to think that we are 'masters of our own ship' and 'charting our own course' in our lives. Whether we are like a lone sailor traversing the world's oceans, or part of a team/crew, is our own choice—despite the needs or hopes of others. We may have to go beyond our deeper fears and take the risk of connecting and relating with others, and of travelling as part of a team—albeit perhaps a small team—in order to fully experience the richness of our individual life.

In order to feel comfortable when alone and not suffer the ache of loneliness we may need to 'adopt' the lonely Child within us, and to show that child the attention, interest, love, respect and guidance it yearns for; to play and have fun; to find a way out of the darkness of loneliness and to skip into the sunlight. So, become your own 'parent', and also be your own best friend. Be the person who will never let you down. Be the loving guardian of your own happiness and you will never walk alone.

Paradoxically the spiritual seekers and quantum scientists tell us that ultimately, at both the sub-atomic and soul levels we are all part of the same one-ness of consciousness anyway; we are all flames in the fire, all waves in the vast ocean, and that we can never truly be alone.

What Do You Mean?

We all think and expect that our shared language enables us to communicate clearly with one another—and of course it does, up to a point. However what we think we are saying may not be what the other person picks up and responds to. We all 'filter' everything in our own way, based upon our unique history, what we expect from others, and what we project onto them—'as-if' they meant what we think they meant. I am sure you will have had countless experiences of this yourself, when someone responded to you in a way that just didn't 'fit' with what you were saying, or what you actually meant, and you then felt like the conversation had somehow become disjointed and side-tracked, leaving you feeling baffled or just surprised. Words can bring clarity, but they can also limit and overwhelm us too. Some people even use language as a way to induce others to feel inferior, or lacking in literary and grammatical education—as a type of one-up-manship-power-game.

Of course, the ways in which our parents, teachers, and other influential people from our past, communicated with us will have 'modelled' their style to us; and we may later copy this style, without even realising it. We do so in order to 'fit-in' and not to stand out as 'different' from the rest of the group. Being perceived as too 'different' might mean rejection, humiliation and ridicule—all of which induce the powerful and disabling emotion of shame within us.

We may have blocks that prevent us from expressing ourselves clearly—perhaps with certain people or in certain settings. This can be caused by low self-esteem/worth, feelings of shame and inadequacy, guilt, and feeling negatively judged, oppressed or intimidated by others. Much of this will simply be our faulty sub-conscious programming and the associated belief-system we have been carrying around for too many years. The other person may indeed be judging you, or trying to dominate, intimidate or oppress you; you may even sub-consciously 'invite' this if it is familiar and fits in with your Life-Script about yourself.

We assume that because we are 'grown-ups' that we automatically should know how to express ourselves effectively and appropriately; but unless we were taught and shown this way of communicating it will be alien to us. Without learning how to speak like an assertive adult we can be confined to childlike and emotionally-based ***reactions*** to people, instead of showing a more rational and considered ***response*** to them. The latter is much more empowering and effective!

There are different levels of communicating—from shallow chit-chat, through the levels of empathy and self-disclosure and right down to the deep and heartfelt way of sharing our innermost world. It is said that small minds talk about other people; medium minds talk about events; and great minds talk about ideas and concepts.

Most of us usually stay in the safe zone of 'small-talk', gossip and the reporting upon situations and events, for most of the time. We may also watch television programmes and read magazines that support this level of communicating too. We tend to reserve the deeper levels of self-expression for fewer and fewer people, if indeed anyone at all. We may seek deeper contact, communication and intimacy—both to give and receive these—but many people haven't experienced these before and it can therefore feel like a foreign and alien language, and way of being, to them.

Some people speak in a way that cancels-out either themselves or the other person, by being overly passive and placating, or by being dominant or overly intellectual. Neither way is effective or helpful as they don't allow people to 'connect' and really communicate as equals.

There are also common errors in everyday speech that we learn from our families and peer groups—meaningless phrases are all too often sprinkled into what we say, and which neither clarify or enhance it, and are just bad habits that are seldom challenged by ourselves or others. The most common is probably the use of the word 'You' instead of 'I'—which is a way of disowning something and getting distance from it perhaps because it causes embarrassment, or because the speaker isn't really connected to their experience—e.g. 'you think to yourself, what a mess you're in and you wonder how you'll ever get out of it'.....instead of 'I thought to myself etc.'

We mustn't forget the communication we have with ourselves too. We all have an inner dialogue going on about most things, most of the time. How we speak to ourselves is very telling and can add to the restrictions and blocks we have in communicating with other people. What we say to ourselves inside determines what we say and do on the outside. We always recreate 'out there' what is 'in here'—until such time as we examine and change the sub-conscious script beliefs and negative inner dialogues. We will need professional help to do this, as the sub-conscious mind cannot be changed by the conscious mind/will or talking therapies alone.

We mustn't forget that we also all have 'sub-personalities' inside us, which each have their own speech patterns, styles and mannerisms, and any one of which can show up and 'take centre stage' in our life-dramas—and not always in a desirable and helpful way. There's so much more to what we say, and how we say it, than we probably ever realised!

When we have cleared away enough of the blocks and learned how to speak cleanly and clearly with our assertive, calm and rational Adult minds—then all of our conversations greatly improve.

Starting a sentence with I...see/hear/think/imagine/want/need/prefer is both empowering and assertive and much more likely to result in a clearer exchange than the usual manipulating, shaming, blaming, and critical or meandering dialogue we are all so familiar with.

So, be mindful of what you really intend to say, and how you say it.

Are Your Moods Getting Other People Down?

We may be so consumed by our own worries, fears and frustrations that we don't realise how our moods and behaviours impact upon other people—and how this in turn can damage our relationships, as well as our home or work environments.

As a boss/manager/leader you may have the illusion of social competence and of being admired and respected by your peers and colleagues for your 'no-nonsense' approach or for 'not suffering fools gladly' or for 'taking no prisoners'. But that may not be what is said about you behind your back!

We are all impacted and affected by the moods of those around us—whether that be the moods of just one person with whom we have regular contact; or the emotional cloud of a group, crowd or mob. The term for this is **Emotional Contagion**—and it can be seen on a large scale in the jubilation of the winning crowd; in national mourning for a beloved public figure; and the mob violence, looting and destruction seen across the country (particularly the riot scenes of summer 2011), and in many places of civil unrest around the world.

We are all connected 'energetically' and we all affect one another—whether we mean to or not. As adults we must take responsibility for our moods and find an effective way to balance them and to live a calmer, happier life.

Due to our life experiences, we may be plagued with feelings of guilt and/or shame; fear of failure, humiliation and rejection; resentment and hostility; self-loathing; jealousy/envy; anger/rage; and more. Any of these is a heavy weight to carry—but we cannot expect others to carry these for us and to have to change their behaviour in order to accommodate our psychological and emotional imbalances!

The patience of any happy, loving, considerate and thoughtful person will be severely tested by being 'infected' by the chronic anxiety, despondency, apathy, shame, guilt, envy, neuroses, victim-hood, anger, aggression, dominance, or bullying from another person..... particularly within close relationships or with work colleagues.

We can use an analogy here of wavelength frequencies—those on a similar wavelength to us resonate with, enrich and vitalise our lives; those on consistently lower frequencies drain our energy and resources and impair our experience of life. We may have to make a 'tough-love' decision not to be around such people if they are unwilling to learn how to change their moods, improve their behaviours, and raise their frequency when around us.

We all have a tendency to 'stress-bond' too. That means we find people with similar grievances/hurts/fears as our own, and then have 'circular conversations' to mutually offload and maybe even seek advice from another 'like-minded' person about our relationships/business concerns etc. This advice, however well-meaning, can only be a reflection of the other person's own unique history and belief system, and will therefore probably not 'fit' for you in your own personal experience of life. Indeed it may make things worse!

So, unless you want your colleagues, partner, children, and others tip-toeing around so as not to 'rock your boat' you will have to find the courage to do something about your infectious emotionality before it reaches the level of contagion!

Unhealthy and dysfunctional behaviours tend to be driven by deeper unexpressed needs, and these will benefit from being acknowledged, known and met. You are the only person who can do this, although an objective, empathic and supportive professional therapist may be of help to you.

> Ask yourself how you would feel if you had to work, or live with 'you', your moods and your behaviours.
>
> How light and easy are you to be around?
>
> What old stuff is getting in your way and blocking you from sharing your best with those around you?
>
> What type of ripple effect do you want to be a part of?

Who you are, both to yourself and to others is up to you. It is your responsibility. Clean yourself up on the inside and you can then radiate a better you to the outside. Others will be pleased you did!

APPEARANCES **C**AN **B**E **D**ECEPTIVE!

We would all like to think that we could take another person 'at face value'—that what we see is what we get. To a certain extent this is true; but there's more to consider.

Our human survival has depended upon our ability to assess, and deal with, any potential threats to our well-being. We 'fill in the gaps'—the things we don't actually know about another person—as an attempt to give us a 'clearer picture' of the sort of person we are dealing with, and how much of a threat they represent to us. We may 'pigeon-hole' someone as a way of creating the illusion for ourselves that we know just what sort of person they are. We might 'project' onto someone else any of our own negative characteristics, which we dislike or even deny the existence of, and then use these as a reason to dislike the other person. We also 'attribute' motives onto other people based upon the partial information we have about them, the most obvious being their appearance and demeanour—how they look and act. Conversely we might project positive qualities onto others that we feel that we also possess ourselves, in an attempt to create a form of kinship and alliance with them. Or instead we might project onto someone the very qualities we wish we had ourselves, and then we admire these in the other person, as if they really existed.

These projections are all based upon our own inner psychological concepts and are not the 'truth'. We can never know the whole truth about anyone, or about anything for that matter. This projection can happen extremely quickly in a first meeting and be based upon our very limited perception or scant information about the other. The other person may just happen to have a certain mannerism, or physical similarity, to someone else we know or used to know. We then treat them 'as-if' they were just like this other person from our history. We 'transfer' or overlay attributes onto them that don't really exist. This then clouds the way in which we attempt to relate to them; or we may not even bother trying to get to know them—as we have convinced ourselves that we 'know just what they're like'.

Our projection and transference of imaginary aspects onto another person is a two-way street. People may well be doing just that to you too! If you feel as though someone is relating negatively to you, or refusing to engage with you, you could ask them if you remind them of someone else they know; and tell them that you are forming the impression that they may be mistaking you for another person and treating you 'as-if' you were that person without taking the time to experience who you really are.

However, who any of us 'really is' isn't fixed anyway. We all change our opinions, values, and sometimes our beliefs and ways of behaving—particularly as a result of our ongoing education and experiences. We can never truly know another person in the way that would help us to feel fully safe and trusting of them. We have to settle for only knowing them clearly 'enough' to be able to decide what level of relationship, if any, we do want to have with them.

A further level in this process is called 'counter-transference'; whereby we react to others based upon what they are projecting onto us. This can be in the form of sub-consciously acting out the part in their life-drama that they have 'assigned' to us; or at least in being aware of their invitation that we become a member of the cast in the replay of their history. Counter-transference can also exist in our responding to them from our own history and experiences; when we then overlay the interaction with them with something from our own past, and then behave 'as-if' it were true and valid in the present day.

Counter-transference can be used 'diagnostically' by a psychotherapist, when they become aware of what is being evoked in them by the client they are working with. Then they must examine if their invited reaction is from their own past history or from that of the client. When sensitively brought into the therapy session, this can be useful in getting to the bottom of a client's underlying issue that needs to be worked with, rather than the issues that are presented on the surface.

When we were children we became aware of how we felt in response to the individuals around us. With some people we felt light and comfortable, whilst with others we may have felt afraid and our body would have tightened and recoiled from them. We will have learned to develop, and convincingly wear, 'masks' with these people so as to present an acceptable 'false self' to them.

All such deeper responses and ways of relating can show themselves in the psychotherapy sessions too, and a skilled therapist will pick up their own feelings from the interaction with the client. The therapist may, for instance, feel like a cold, critical, and demeaning mother; or perhaps a dominant bully; or maybe feel bored, tired, and disinterested in the client. These are all indicators of either the client's, or the therapists, history. The therapist should therefore have undergone their own long-term therapy to have dealt with their own history and projections/transferences, and to not act them out with their clients—who deserve this level of professionalism and clarity from their sessions.

The nugget in all of this is in knowing that deeper sub-conscious levels of perception do exist between everyone, and that we cannot really take anyone, or indeed can ourselves be taken, 'at face value' after all!

WHAT ARE YOUR BOUNDARIES AND RESPONSIBILITIES?

These two words can represent a vague and often troublesome area of our lives. Where are your boundaries? And what, and whom, are you responsible for?

Your personal boundaries are obviously not fixed and solid like a fence or a wall. Instead they are an expression of your personal comfort and preferences. You may have different boundaries with different people in different situations and may not even be aware of these boundaries until they are challenged and threatened. Healthy boundaries affirm us as individuals and say to others 'this point is OK with me—and beyond that point isn't OK with me'.

As individuals we can have boundaries in our lives around such aspects as: my time, and what I'm willing to share of this with another; my levels of personal disclosure; how far I will put myself out for this particular person at this time; my sexual boundaries with this person; my workplace or job description boundaries; and my financial boundaries and what I will spend, borrow or repay.

It can be difficult even to know how to set a boundary with someone, let alone how to maintain it and ensure that it isn't crossed. This goes hand in hand with being an assertive adult, and knowing that you have the right to express what you want, need and prefer, as well as what you are experiencing; and most importantly what sense you make of that experience and what you imagine it means.

We don't have to be too rigid about our boundaries, and it can be worthwhile checking-in with ourselves if we still want an existing boundary to remain in the same place with a certain person or situation. We can change these 'settings' as time and experiences unfold.

We will have learned about boundaries, or lack of them, in our childhood. Having had parents/caregivers whose boundaries were too loose and vague, or too rigid and unyielding will have left its impact upon us and the sub-conscious decisions we will have made about protecting ourself from the manipulation, domination, and intrusion of other people. These decisions might no longer fit into your modern-day adult world.

It can be easier to soften boundaries that are too rigid—as we learn to trust ourselves to be able to deal with any threats to them—than it is to find the 'raw materials' with which to attempt to build new boundaries from scratch, when we don't have the know-how or experience of how to do this.

You are responsible for your own boundaries—where they are and how firm they are. You are not responsible for the boundaries of others or for trying to change them—that's down to them and their own personal history and level of awareness.

Similarly, you are not responsible for anyone else's feelings. You are, however, responsible for the way in which you communicate with and deal with other people, but not for their feelings. Those are created by the other person's own belief system and personal history. As long as you are fair, clear, honest and consistent, then that is your half of the responsibility in a relationship. The only exception to that relates to children. We do have a responsibility *for* them as well as *towards* them; but other adults must take responsibility for themselves and for their own life experiences.

We have all experienced 'difficult' people who push our boundaries, and encourage us to push theirs too—as they 'play out their dramas' with us. To name a few, these people could be the Interrogator, the Guilt-Tripper, the Drama Queen/King, the Egotist, the Manipulator, the Control Freak, the Martyr/Sufferer, the Bully, the Narcissist, and the Crazy Chaotic. They present us with a lot of boundary threats! How do we deal with these people?

We must be crystal clear with them about what we see, hear and imagine they mean. We must not bluff or patronise; and we must follow through on promises or ultimatums. It's for their own good and is actually modelling the good, fair and respectful boundaries they may not have had when they were children. In all probability, they will not give up their behaviours just like that, and will no doubt persist in trying to weaken your boundaries—which if successful would be detrimental to both parties.

Those people who don't take responsibility for themselves create dramas that they attempt to pull other people into. They have their own way of perceiving events and ways of reacting which will often be neurotic and irrational. Hard as it might be, it can be helpful to encourage these people to 'feel' and share their feelings—as long as it isn't part of a Victim/Rescuer dynamic that they are trying to play out with you!

If we can empathise with the pain of the 'wounded child' in another person—and we all have one—we can connect more from our heart, whilst still relying upon our rational-adult head to give us an understanding of their behaviour, and of course, to maintain our much needed boundaries with them.

Jealousy and Envy

A dictionary definition of jealousy describes feelings of 'hostility towards someone thought of as a rival, and involves resentment, anxiety and the scrutiny of that rival.' Envy is defined as 'resentment or discontent at other's achievements or possessions'. In common everyday language we tend to use the words in a wider context, with jealousy also being interchanged and used synonymously with envy. We all feel some degree of jealousy and envy. It can be something useful to spur us on to achieve our own greatness in some way.

When we hear someone described as being jealous, we usually mean that they are afraid. Afraid of losing the love, care, and attention of either someone valued as 'special' to them; or of losing someone who is needed by an insecure or controlling person to meet their own needs. We can all become afraid of another man/woman taking an interest in our partner or friend, and fear that this other person may in some way entice or seduce our partner, or friend, away from us.

It may be that they have the attention and interest of our partner, and we wish we had that all to ourself, to help us to feel safer about the relationship. This 'jealousy' is really just insecurity and fear, perhaps with good reason. Some partners behave in ways that create insecurity and doubt, and they make relationships feel temporary, and lacking in honesty and commitment. We might fear the pain of loss, and perhaps also the shame and indignity of being seen as not-as-good-as the person who 'replaces' us in our partner's/friend's life. Such fear drives some people to control and manipulate others, in a desperate attempt to avoid losing them. Sadly this usually only results in driving them away!

Some people may use such a scenario—the loss, or potential loss, of someone they are emotionally attached to—to reinforce their own negative self-belief system. Others will overcompensate by making desperate efforts to enhance their appearance and find themselves a 'replacement' partner/lover to make their 'ex' feel this so-called jealousy; in the hope that their 'ex' will realise their mistake and come back to them. If this manipulation were successful it would then open up a new aspect of the relationship—that of learning how to trust and respect a person again following the pain of earlier betrayal and rejection by them.

In personal and couple psychotherapy sessions the pain and anguish of a jealous/possessive/needy person is tangible. The fear of the loss of their partner, or someone else they are strongly attached to, can be brought back into perspective by strengthening their self-esteem, and helping them to form, or re-claim, a more balanced and robust sense of their own value, positive attributes and accomplishments, and by developing an ability to cope with difficult emotions and circumstances. They will need to regain their own sense of power and potency and not have to rely upon another person for their positive self-image and feelings of well-being. This is called 'internal validation'—we learn to validate ourselves, and not to need someone else to be doing this for us.

Hell has no fury like a woman scorned/spurned, as they say, and recent reports in the media tell us of celebrity wives, and even the wife of a leading political figure, 'making things difficult' for their former partner by using the media to publicly shame them as a form of punishment for infidelity and betrayal. This revenge applies to both genders, and recently the media has also reported that several 'jealous', or rather obsessed and possessive, husbands/partners have used 'jealousy and provocation' as their 'defence' against the murder, or attempted murder of their wife or partner—who perhaps had a lover; or who wanted to separate from them or to divorce them. This obviously far exceeds jealousy. It is evidence of a pathological rage and shame at a perceived rejection and abandonment. Rage that has all too often ended in violence or death, not only directed towards a spouse or partner but also, sadly, their innocent children too.

Men tend to compete with other men when it comes to sport/work/status/wealth and the sex-appeal of their wives/partners. Women tend to be particularly envious of one another's physical prowess, although some women have given up comparing themselves to other women because they believe that they never can come out on top. We women usually try to hide our jealousy and envy of another woman's beauty, sex-appeal, intelligence, charisma, power and wealth. Instead we tend to criticise, ridicule, and demean the envied woman. We may even wish that we could somehow rob her of her 'attributes'. If we are in the fortunate position of having such assets and attributes ourselves then that puts us on a good solid footing. Plenty of research shows that we are then likely to be responded to more positively and benevolently, by society in general, than would happen if we didn't have these 'benefits'. But with this comes the jealousy, envy, and resentment of the competitive women around us. The one 'leveller' in all of this female jealousy and envy is ageing. As we age, generally speaking, even the most beautiful become less so, although some develop a different type of beauty—and there is always the 'compensation' of being seen as 'good-for-your-age'!

Those who have a need to appear young and desirable, for longer than nature allows, can pay for cosmetic enhancements which may be either subtle or disfiguring. The latter certainly don't arouse jealousy or envy. A woman who wants to be admired and envied for her beauty can thus rob herself of this very asset through too much cosmetic surgery, and instead evoke pity and ridicule. In the professional world the older woman becomes less visible—unless she is the business owner/founder/figure-head—who can be respected, admired and revered.

Anyone achieving success may well be envied, and their competitors may then try to even-the-playing-field by engaging in ridicule, shame-inducing revelations, criticism, theft of ideas, and copy-cat tactics. If someone lacks the intelligence, skill, courage, self-belief and integrity to succeed on their own merits, they may try to take the 'short-cut' of copying someone else's successful ideas and business strategies. Jealousy and envy can bring out the worst in us.

Most people want to be happy, and they probably equate happiness with wealth, material goods, beauty, power and status. Many people try to buy happiness and love. Our preoccupation with the celebrity culture only enforces this and makes slaves of the fame-seekers, and money-chasers. We live in a society of instant gratification. We want it all, and we want it now—and we feel jealous and envious of those who already have what we want.

The way to avoid the pitfalls of jealousy and envy is to remind yourself of what you do have! We all have at least something that someone else might feel jealous or envious about—even if it's just our voice, eye colour or hairstyle! Even better if it is our character traits, personality, success or something else we have had control over and have developed for ourselves. Being grateful and counting your blessings helps to re-balance the scales and helps us to realise that we are indeed blessed—even though on the gloomy days it may not seem that way. Look and you *will* find these flecks of gold in the rock that makes up your present life.

For those who are more spiritually inclined, there is a release from these chains of craving, jealousy, envy and possessiveness—which all stem from the fear of 'not-having', and of not being 'good-enough'. The more spiritually-enlightened realise that nothing is permanent, that everything is relative, connected and transient; and that happiness doesn't come from outside, or from desiring and possessing objects, or from beauty, wealth or by keeping people emotionally entangled with you.

In this more spiritual way of life lies greater freedom......and that is something we should, paradoxically perhaps, all feel envious of!

<u>Robust Self-Esteem—The Greatest Gift of All!</u>

At birthdays and Christmas time we become focussed upon what gifts we could give to our own family and friends. There is one gift that we can give all year round, it costs us nothing and yet is priceless as it affects both the receiver and everyone else they come into contact with. The gift is that of healthy, positive and robust self-esteem—most importantly for our children!

We may not have this already for ourselves and so we find it difficult to know how to 'pass it on' to our children—but it is our profound duty to find, nurture and strengthen our own self-worth, for humanity's sake. I think the most vital gifts we can give to our children are good self-esteem and an ability to regulate their emotional states. These will be of immense value for a whole lifetime—long after a trendy toy or gadget has lost its appeal!

Males tend to derive their self-esteem or self-worth from a sense of achievement and success, such as in sporting, academic or career outlets. Whereas females tend to find it through social interactions and acceptance. Unfortunately, if our sense of 'worth' is dependant upon external factors such as wealth, beauty, career promotions, designer labels etc. it can just as easily be swept away when these aspects of our lives are no longer there.

What do you imagine it would it feel like to really and truly respect, value, like and admire yourself? How would you walk, talk, dress, and, most importantly, behave with other people?

Some people appear to have high self-esteem but it is really a cover-up for feeling depleted and not good-enough, and they 'compensate' for this by being boastful, arrogant or even narcissistic. Those with genuine high-self-esteem don't need to express any such behaviours.

We are all affected by our experiences—right from the time we are in the womb. We can be born with a 'tendency' to be more cautious and withdrawn; and if this becomes overlaid with negative life experiences then our self-belief is skewed towards a negative and pessimistic view of ourselves. We are all very impressionable in childhood and we absorb critical and hurtful comments, disapproving looks, rejections and ridicule without being able to validate or evaluate them. We just believe them to be true and valid because the 'big people' who run our lives say it is so; and we pick up and internalise these messages from them many thousands of times. A child can come to see themselves as unworthy, unlovable, flawed, and defective in some way. They can feel like an outsider in their own family as if they don't 'belong' there and are not wanted. Particularly if they have also experienced physical or emotional trauma, abuse or neglect.

Our sub-conscious and 'core' belief system is largely in place by the time we are six years old; and we then re-create and filter events and situations which serve to re-enforce these often erroneous beliefs. We get stuck in a downward spiral of self doubt, feelings of incompetence and lack of worth or value. Maybe even self-loathing and a desire to re-create self-punishment, and to ensure that we have to struggle for survival in our later lives.

Until we understand how we came to be who we are today and to make sense of the factors that have shaped us; we may be doomed to both recreating the earlier 'dramas' we've experienced (in the hope of changing the ending); or to keep ourselves imprisoned in a cell—without realising the door isn't actually locked. We have the means to free ourselves and to become who we were fully meant to be. To live a fulfilling and meaningful life. To have happy and growthful relationships, and most importantly, to guide our children to do the same!

You can start today by committing to clear away the negative effects of the inadequate parenting you may have received; and learn to like, respect and admire yourself for the progress you have made in getting to where you are now. Motivate yourself as you would your own child. Give credit where it is due, and celebrate successes. Have clear and self-affirming boundaries that allow you to express your needs, desires and preferences. Show compassion, empathy, courage, and love wherever you can. Become the parent that your child will be proud to emulate. Give freely of your time to your child and show them how to create a good life for themselves by teaching them how to think positively, feel from their heart and touch others with their love.

'Til Debt Us Do Part? How Strong is Your Relationship?

Recent newspaper articles and television reports have highlighted an increase in divorce rates which, they claim, is attributed to the 'recession'. How do we know this is the reason? How much can we trust and believe the statistics presented to us? What about the relationships of non-married couples? How does this 'news' affect your view of your own relationship?

Finances are just one part of the complexity that is a 'relationship'. We all bring into a relationship our own beliefs about money, which are based upon what we saw, heard and experienced in childhood relating to money and abundance, wealth, poverty and scarcity. Money means different things to different people. For some it can equate to power and status—which may be sought and needed to bolster a shaky self-esteem; for others it is a means of providing material comforts for loved ones; and for all of us it gives us greater choices—about what we eat, what we buy, where we live, and how we spend our leisure time etc. Money can give us an illusion of 'security' too, and some people 'marry for money' as a 'trade-off' for love and genuine connection and affection with a partner.

If marriages are indeed ending because of restricted finances surely this calls into question the foundation of those relationships. It can be cheaper to be living with someone than having to meet all household outgoings alone; so maybe the reason for this increase in divorce rates is not really about a lack of money.

Deciding to become separated or divorced can bring intensely painful feelings. Our brains register emotional pain similar to the way they register physical pain, and it can 'feel' as though we have had a part of us physically ripped away. We will have developed an 'attachment' to our PAP—Primary Attachment Person—too and that attachment can take time and effort to weaken before we feel free to embark upon another relationship.

There are many different types of relationship and many different reasons for them to break-up. Relationships offer us a way of growing as a person as we learn to compromise, respectfully deal with conflict, to share and care for another, and to get some of our basic human needs met too. It is surprising that we aren't educated more about relationships when we are in our early teens—they are so fundamental to us and they can so easily go wrong if we don't understand them, or our role in them. Our early experiences with relationships were probably based upon physical attraction and the power/status/prestige/popularity of our partner. Maybe we saw in our partner aspects missing in ourself and we had the fantasy that being with them would somehow make us feel 'complete'. Many people simply 'played-safe' and settled for someone who wanted them—and thereby avoided being alone .... in one sense at least. Loneliness whilst in a relationship is very painful too.

Our brains are not mature until we are about 25 years old (and they continue to evolve as we encounter new experiences); and yet we are conditioned into making significant and life-changing decisions about our relationships and sometimes, even about having children of our own (a big challenge to any relationship), before this age.

Many of us do not even know what a good healthy relationship looks like, as we haven't experienced it during our own childhood. We may have had poor relationships modelled to us by our parents—which may lead us to avoid the commitment of relationships altogether; or we may become determined to make a poor relationship work out—despite mounting evidence to the contrary!

In our current times of temporary and disposable 'virtual' friends and 'cyber-relationships' we can loose sight of what a good relationship could bring us. We have to remind ourselves what it is that we really want and need from a relationship. There needs to be a real respect and love for our partner—warts and all; and a mutual desire to be emotionally connected with one another. Lack of these is a common reason for break-ups.

As human beings we all have a profound need to be wanted, accepted, understood, to feel that we are valued and that we 'belong'; to have someone stable to rely upon, and for them to be able to rely upon us too; someone to fight our corner and watch our backs; someone to laugh and play with; we want so much just to love and be loved. It's only in our later years that we even think about our compatibility with a partner...when we've had time to get to know our own values and what matters to us in life. No partner is likely to tick all the boxes but we know which boxes we can compromise on and which we can't. This certainly narrows the field! We need our heads as well as our hearts to know 'what will I receive?' as well as 'what can I give and share?', in this relationship?

Sadly, many people are running on fear, and instead of finding a compatible partner, they will 'make-do' and find someone they can merge their identity with. Or find a partner with emotional and psychological problems that they treat as their 'project' for life—these are forms of co-dependency and entanglements, instead of relationships. Some play out Master/Slave or Parent/Child roles too which takes them further away from a healthy and growthful relationship with a respected equal.

Our personal sub-conscious belief system—which is running our lives over 90% of the time—will dictate the relationships we choose and the role we play in them. Fortunately this core belief system can now be changed (see www.qpp.uk.com)

Good relationships are priceless and they give our lives purpose and meaning—and they are not cast aside because of a 'recession'....in fact the times of adversity are the times of greatest growth!

PAIN AND SUFFERING ARE NOT THE SAME THING

We tend to assume that any form of enduring or chronic pain, be it physical or emotional, automatically brings with it a sense of suffering; but the two are not necessarily linked, unless we choose it to be so. Suffering is only a mental concept. How we each perceive our own level of pain, and how this pain then 'fits' into our own belief system about our life and what we expect from it, will affect whether our pain becomes a means of suffering, or not. The symptoms of illness and the experience of pain are always held in the mind either consciously with awareness, or sub-consciously; and as such we can say that all illness and pain is therefore psycho-somatic.

The areas in the brain where we register both our emotional and physical pain are located in the same region, and they can both feel equally real and intense. Chronic pain is associated with an abnormality in the Frontal Cortex of the brain—although pain is registered and filtered at other sites prior to reaching the Frontal Cortex.

There are abundant 'opiate' receptors in the Frontal Cortex of the brain—which is the area responsible for our being able to plan things and making choices—and these receptors receive the body's own mood-enhancing chemicals, called Endorphins, which soothe pain and also evoke states of bliss. These Endorphins are also the peptides for love, bonding and attachment, and the good news is that we can all increase their levels by natural means such as meditation, being in nature, laughing with friends and family, kissing and cuddling. The body makes its own *natural* versions of Valium, Marijuana, Cocaine, Alcohol.....we are 'hard-wired' to feel unity, bliss and love without the use of illicit drugs. You already have your own inner-pharmacy—it just takes the right thoughts and behaviours to open the door!

Our 'pain threshold' is set in a part of the brain called the Peri-acqueductal Gray (PAG); and you have conscious control over the degree of pain you feel, by your thoughts and the words that you use. Your brain is constantly registering every word that you say—and believe to be true—via neuro-peptides (biological messengers) released by the brain and sent throughout your body. These are then accepted by receptors on the cells of every piece of tissue and every organ you have—especially of the nervous and immune system. A 'conversation' is always going on throughout your BodyMind. **You change everything when you change your mind!**

Unfortunately, some people 'need' their suffering for what is called a 'secondary gain'. They elicit care, concern and attention from others which they fear they might not otherwise receive if they weren't ill, in pain, and 'suffering'. For some, their income from the State and other health insurance is dependant upon prolonged illness, and their mindset can ensure that their illness and pain remain a feature of their lives and even, for some, a part of their identity. The subject of their pain and suffering is usually the main topic of their conversations—another 'secondary gain'.

Believing that someone really 'cares' about us when we are ill helps us to heal—assuming that we want to heal of course. The cellular receptors in the body are synchronised and 'entrained' by the care and love of others around us. Doctors and nurses please take note!

Love is real and biochemically measurable—at 528 Hertz (cycles per second). The cascade of neural and biochemical events associated with love, caring and appreciation, affect every organ in the body. The activity of the Sympathetic Nervous System (fight-flight-freeze-flop) is reduced, whilst increasing the 'growth-promoting' and soothing activity of the Para-Sympathetic Nervous System. Production of the stress hormone Cortisol—which has many health-damaging properties—is reduced; and the 'anti-ageing' hormone DHEA is produced instead.

"Love is a universal pattern of resonant energy....the universal harmonic—which has the power to heal even cancerous tumours" (Laskow)

"Love, compassion and relationships heal us and lead to greater recovery from disease" (Candace Pert).

Placebos work because heartfelt belief activates the body's own innate healing system. Nocebos work too; if we believe that bad, negative things will befall us—they will do so. You get what you believe!

Smiling reduces the secretion of stress hormones, and raises the production of Endorphins (the 'feel-good' chemicals); as well as enhancing the function of the T-cells of the Immune System. Frowning has the opposite effect—as well as raising blood pressure, and increasing your susceptibility to anxiety and depression. So remember that the next time you catch sight of your reflection—and change a miserable frown into a radiant smile!

We get what we focus upon. If you focus on pain and how awful and unfair it is to you, then you will feel it to be magnified and greater than it really is. If you are able to acknowledge any pain you may have, and accept that it is just one aspect of your current life, then this positive outlook reduces its impact and frees you up to focus on the more positive, rewarding and supportive things that you will then be able to see all around you.

Pain is inevitable—but the extent to which you allow it to impact upon your life is up to you!

Vicarious Trauma

Have you ever witnessed a traumatic event happening to someone else; or been affected by hearing about it in detail?

We can be impacted by trauma, even though we are not the victim of the trauma. If we are either a witness, or if we sympathise, empathise and offer support and compassion to the victim, then we can be affected by the trauma too. If we witness a traumatic event, the 'mirror neurons' in our brains are activated and we feel, to a certain extent, as if the event had happened to us!

Vicarious trauma is particularly seen in counsellors who repeatedly work with victims of assault, rape, abuse and torture. It is also an occupational hazard for the emergency services—fire-fighters, ambulance staff and paramedics, hospital staff, police officers, and for the armed forces too—when there may be the added emotional and psychological burden of actual bodily trauma and consequent Post Traumatic Stress Disorder—which will need to be worked with using professional help.

Workers in these professions have to learn to 'emotionally numb' themselves to what they experience—in order for them to be able to carry out their work. They have to 'emotionally detach' and become more cognitively focussed upon dealing with the situation. It can then be hard for such professionals to 'switch back on' emotionally with their family and friends when in these safer environments. Some have said that it takes a few days for them to process their 'vicarious trauma' enough to be emotionally available to relate with loved ones fully; by which time they are usually 'back in the firing line' at work. Some also say that they find an escape in alcohol and other 'mood-altering' substances and behaviours, as a way of avoiding their real and overwhelming emotions.

There have been too many cases reported of ex-servicemen suffering with Post-Traumatic Stress Disorder who are not given the help and treatment they need to rebalance their brain after the horrors of war. Seeing horrific events can over-stimulate the emotional part of our brain and affect our daily lives considerably; as can hearing about such events from the victim, who may be your partner or a family member. Many such traumatised people find it very difficult to fit back into society and they can become homeless and have alcohol problems as they try to 'self-medicate' and find a way to avoid the effects of the over-stimulation of their brains. Workers in the voluntary sectors are often not properly trained or qualified to work effectively with these people who have 'slipped through the net' of society, and such workers can themselves suffer from vicarious trauma as they try their best to help.

Traumatised people primarily need to acknowledge that they did survive (although survivor guilt can be an added difficulty for them). They then need to restore a sense of 'safety' in their lives—which is very hard to do if they are homeless, or a refugee. When they feel safe enough, they can then slowly develop a sense of security and comfort. From that platform they can build a feeling of freedom both from the grip of their earlier trauma, and the freedom to make choices that will positively shape their future.

Our news reports always have a new tragedy to inform us about. Graphic images of a murdered dictator, or the recent slaughter of many Syrian children, have been splattered over the front pages of national newspapers. Television news stories of traumatic, tragic and brutal events are often repeated every half hour or more—such as the September 11th 2001 images, and the many subsequent bombings.

So, how are we psychologically affected by exposure to this 'bad news'? The effects are not as great as if we had experienced the trauma personally, but the cumulative effects of second-hand exposure, or of seeing several horrific sights in our day to day lives, also has a huge impact upon our ability to 'process' such material, and to regain our own emotional equilibrium.

Emergency service workers, and counsellors who work with traumatised people, should all have access to their own counselling to enable them to 'offload' the psychological weight of their work and ensure that they don't emotionally 'burn-out'. However, just talking about an event might not be effective enough, as it is our bodies that are impacted by witnessing, or hearing about someone else's trauma in the first instance, and then we think about what happened, and then we find the words for the story we will tell about it. With vicarious trauma we will not have had our body impacted with anything like the same intensity as the actual victim, but we will have thoughts, images, emotions and bodily sensations linked to what we see or hear.

It can be very difficult to be in a relationship with someone who has been directly traumatised—whether that be unresolved childhood trauma or a more recent accident or assault. The person will 'change' in both their perceptions and behaviours. You may feel that you don't 'know' them any longer. You may feel that being around them and their pain is too overwhelming and only a sense of love or duty holds you there. You may want to be their support, but may not be able to cope with that burden alone, and will need support of your own either from friends, a self-help group or a professional counsellor or psychotherapist.

The loss or death of a child in whatever circumstances is both a direct and a vicarious trauma which has all too often resulted in a relationship breakdown for the parents. Grief blocks the processing of trauma and the strain takes its toll upon the relationship bond. In such a case each person will need their own separate counselling in addition to later work to repair the relationship, and to form a different relationship in the absence of the child.

We all deal with direct trauma and vicarious trauma in our own way, which will be determined by our own history and our own inner sense of strength and resilience, as well as our willingness to get any help we may need.

Just having an awareness of the existence, and the effects, of vicarious trauma can be a help as we realise just how big a challenge it can be for us all. We can then search for, and hopefully find, the strength, courage and resilience to be present in the face of any further traumas we may encounter, in spite of our fear that they might totally engulf us.

NEW YEAR RESOLUTIONS—WHY BOTHER?

Without wishing to sound negative or pessimistic, there may well be little point in you making such resolutions—because you will probably sabotage them anyway!

Good intentions are one thing—but actual change requires more than these. Maybe, like me in the past, you've been food-shopping and made a conscious choice not to buy chocolate/biscuits/cake—only to 'find' these in your trolley when you reach the checkout. Your sub-conscious mind is running your life over 90% of the time and will always get its own way! You cannot change it from a conscious rational choice to do so....which is why many talking therapies just don't bring deeper and lasting change.

So, back to these Resolutions. These often take the form of 'I won't smoke any more' or 'I won't eat so much' and they appear on the surface at least to be self-affirming and health-promoting. However, the sub-conscious mind will focus on the words 'smoke' and 'eat' and that is what you will do MORE of! Any intentions to change need to be phrased positively and in the present tense, and with heartfelt meaning too; such as 'I now take good care of my body' and 'I give my body what it needs to bring me good health'. This format makes a big difference.....but that's not the end of the matter. If your sub-conscious mind doesn't believe what you are saying or intending then it will sabotage your planned changes and maintain the status-quo. For instance, if it believes that you must be fat in order to feel safe from intimacy or the romantic interests of others, then fat you will stay!

There are other factors that will also influence your weight and health that are not generally publicised and which will also ensure that you keep the fat on. These are 'Inflammation' and 'Toxicity'. Despite what is routinely put out in the media there is more to obesity than just 'too many calories consumed and too little exercise'....that is only a part of the overall picture. If your body is struggling with an acidic and inflamed state, or is under siege from toxins in the environment (such as pesticides), or inner toxicity from Candida, parasites or food intolerances to name a few—then your body will hold onto its fat, to protect both your vital organs, and to store the toxins within the fat.

Similarly, knowing about the health dangers associated with smoking does little to bolster the will-power of the many smokers who try to give up. Difficulty with giving up smoking is not just about nicotine addiction and rituals/habits. Smokers do experience a neuro-chemical reaction from smoking; but they may also need to smoke to mask their emotional difficulties and 'stuff down' their feelings with the long draw-down on a cigarette.

The gamblers, compulsive shoppers, self-harmers, the eating-disordered, and workaholics may 'need' their behaviours in order to get a neuro-chemical 'buzz' in their brains—which temporarily distracts them from their deeper emotional pain. Talking therapies may change behaviours—but these might just be substituted by other dysfunctional behaviours that also provide the Dopamine and Beta-Endorphin release in the brain which they crave. There are healthier and more natural ways of getting this neuro-chemical 'fix'—such as taking certain nutritional supplements, and improving your lifestyle and mindset; but any underlying unmet needs will still need to be understood and alleviated before real change can occur. New Year resolutions are therefore often destined to fail.

The little child you once were still lives inside you. He or she may desperately want to play and have fun, and to be attractive to others, and to have a sense of 'belonging' somewhere. However if the experiences in your life have set up a contradictory sub-conscious belief system, all attempts will fail....and the Inner Child stays stuck, blocked and yearning for change; changes which you won't allow to happen—at least until these deeper core beliefs have first been exposed and changed.

So, in a nutshell......there is little point in making promises to yourself that you cannot keep—this will only reinforce your feelings of failure and negative self-image.

For lasting change at a deeper level we need to change these all important sub-conscious beliefs about ourself, about what we deserve and how our life will be. We must change the 'Script' of our life and the characters and outcome of our Life Drama will then change too.

Happy New Year? Will You Allow it to Be?

We all hear and say 'Happy New Year' so often in late December and early January each year, but rarely do we think about what it really means to us, and the people to whom we say it.

We are all unique individuals with our own needs and desires; and most of us are united in our quest for the same thing—to feel happy. We are all striving for this state of 'happiness'; and yet many people are looking for it in the wrong place, and instead they are settling for a temporary mood-enhancer in the form of alcohol, drugs, a new relationship, or new possessions.

At that time of year the magazines are full of 'New Year New You' advice from so-called experts—most of which is just plain common sense. No one else is the expert on you! Only you know—or are trying to pin-down—what brings you personal happiness. One person's happiness is another person's burden.

If you now think about what actually brings different people happiness it might range from: finding shelter and food; having a make-over/fake-tan/fake-nails etc.; buying new 'toys/gadgets'; right through to showing love, care and compassion to others. As broad a spectrum as is seen in general society. Happiness for you will depend upon your own level of personal and spiritual awareness, and your ability to create happiness as a state of mind which you can return to at will—despite life's relentless disappointments and challenges. It is not enough to simply 'think' or 'imagine' yourself as being happy—you can't fool yourself that easily for very long!

What most of us don't realise is that we all have two mind-sets about everything in our own life, and these 'two minds' can be at odds with one another. This conflict can include the levels and quality of happiness we 'allow' ourselves to experience. Our conscious/rational/observing mind can desire and seek greater happiness, but if the sub-conscious mind doesn't believe that we deserve it, or that we would benefit from it—then it just isn't going to come our way. Our outer lives are only ever a reflection of our inner and deeper sub-conscious belief system. Self-help books and the conventional talking therapies do not access or change these deeper 'script' beliefs.

Being around happy, optimistic, warm and friendly people positively affects us too—as does the opposite. This is known as 'Emotional Contagion' and it is worth reflecting upon what mood or 'energy' we ourselves give out that in turn affects those around us. We all have specific neurons in our brains called Mirror Neurons, which can create in us the emotion that we are witnessing outside of ourselves. For instance if we see someone stub their toe or trap their finger, we are instinctively programmed to feel something similar. This connection goes beyond mere 'empathy', or of recalling personal memories of similar things having happened to us in the past. We are significantly and positively affected by being around happy events and happy people, because we can then 'mirror' these happy and positive emotions within ourselves. There is a 'ripple-effect' amongst us as we share such energy between us—so we might as well make it positive energy and a positive ripple!

However, don't be fooled by a 'happy mask' that someone may be wearing, which will be a false-self they present to the world as an attempt to hide their real feelings and needs. This may well have been set up in childhood when it was encouraged and expected that they 'put-on-a-happy face' for the family's sake; and to stuff down their real feelings such as anger, resentment, disappointment, fear, sadness and despair—which was real, but regarded as 'unacceptable' by the family/care-giver. Many people are so accustomed to wearing a mask that they cannot imagine a life without it, or even know how to take it off! Their eyes will usually give the game away as to their true underlying feelings, as will a verbal slip or shift in facial expression in an unguarded moment, if another person is sensitive enough to notice these of course.

We all have a 'base-line' level of happiness at any given stage in our lives—which is formed from our past experiences and the meaning we gave to them; and of course the effects these have had upon our sub-conscious mind and the 'programme' we are running. This base-line represents only 50% of the full amount of happiness we are capable of experiencing at the present time. A further 10% can come from the external 'lucky' events such as a lottery win, or a big new purchase, or from cosmetic surgery etc. These 'highs' are unfortunately only temporary and we soon return to our base level once again. The very good news though is that the remaining 40% of happiness available to you—is derived from YOU! This is scientifically validated and forms a central aspect of Positive Psychology.

There are several ways of facilitating more happiness by your own actions and thoughts, and by the releasing of your own blocks to true happiness. These ways include learning how to develop a more optimistic and focussed approach to life; to maintaining your healthy mind and spirit, and allowing gratitude and forgiveness into your life. These sound simple but are in fact profound and life-changing. Improving and sustaining your overall happiness positively affects every cell in your body and consequently your health and your lifespan.

Deeper and sustained happiness equates to a calmness of the mind; of observing what is, and not forcing change; of reflecting, surrendering and allowing, instead of worrying, over-thinking and mind-chatter; of knowing that things will turn out as you have designed them, and that you have designed them as best you know how at this point in your life. To see the pleasure in every tiny moment instead of only focussing ahead, or dwelling on the unchangeable past. The only time you really have is this moment and the next breath. Make the most of these whilst you still have them.

So perhaps instead of the customary and thoughtless 'Happy New Year' to one and all—it would be more relevant to say 'May You Find and Sustain Your Own Happiness' .....ah, but that's too much of a mouthful... it'll probably never catch on!

IS YOUR MEMORY RELIABLE?

No it isn't.

A survey carried out in August 2011 by the University of Illinois, found that of the 1,500 people surveyed, most people thought that their memory was as reliable as a video camera, and they also thought that their memories never changed.

In fact, according to research by John Seamon, (professor of psychology and neuroscience) at Wesleyan University, Connecticut, our memory is wrong in about a third of cases. Furthermore, the more frequently we recall an event, the less accurately we remember it. This happens because when we recall a particular memory our brain does not go back to the event itself, but to the last time we recalled it. Each recollection and reconstruction adds new flaws and reinforces previous flaws. We then 'settle' on a version that we consider to be the 'truth'. After about a year of doing this, Seamon adds, the memory and its flaws solidifies and becomes the person's 'constant truth'.

These are particularly interesting research findings when related to our memory of a crime, divorce and the earlier relationship history, or something else that we may subsequently be 'swearing an oath' to 'tell the truth' about, perhaps several years afterwards.

Some people repeatedly and intentionally recall bad memories as a way of reinforcing negative beliefs about themselves and their lives; as if to prove their tragic life-script to be true.

In psychotherapy circles the issue of 'false memory' has been discussed over recent years. Some clients have felt that they were induced by a therapist/hypnotherapist to have a memory of abuse that didn't actually happen to them. Whilst this is indeed a terrible notion, it should not deter the public from working with a fully trained, experienced and knowledgeable therapist. Real memories have an emotional undertone to them—false memories do not.

A memory is only a 'bringing of the past into the present', and it can therefore be very useful to reminisce about good, nostalgic, sentimental events that we have experienced as this can raise our level of happiness and well-being in the present time.

Alcohol and drug use adversely effects our ability to remember things. They both interfere with our sleep patterns and the storage and retrieval of memory. Being drunk or 'high' usually leaves the user with big blanks, instead of memories, of the previous events—which may include harmful, distressing and even criminal elements within them.

Emotional, psychological and physical traumas can shut-down and block access to our memories. Nightmares can be a way of processing trauma, but if the memory of the experience is too traumatic even these nightmares will be blocked, to protect the person from recalling a horrible event.

In a therapeutic assessment session, I ask a new client if their memories are consistent in time or if there are any periods for which they have no memory. Sometimes a client will say something like 'I have no memory before the age of six years' or ' I have a blank between the ages of nine and 13 years' for instance. This may indicate that trauma has been experienced during these times, which has blocked the memory as a way of avoiding acknowledgement of what happened.

However we cannot recall anything verbally prior to the age of about three years—which was when our left-brain language and cognitive centres became sufficiently developed. Abuse, trauma, or neglect prior to the age of three years will have been 'stored' in physical sensations and images only, but with no 'story' attached to them. Psychotherapeutic work which focusses upon the body—where trauma is stored—can be used to access and process these very early, intrinsic and somatic memories.

We have both 'explicit' and 'implicit' memories; as well as both short-term and long-term memory functions. Explicit memories are those that can be expressed in language such as a place name or a book title. Implicit memories are the memories that you are not consciously aware of—such as how to drive your car or how to tie a shoe lace.

Short-term memory allows us to recall something for a few minutes—like the name of a person we've just been introduced to—whereas with repetition, long-term memory allows us to recall this years later. When we revise for exams, or learn to drive a car, we repeat short-term memory input until it becomes long-term memory which is then available to us for as long as we continue to recall it—even if only from time to time.

Short-term memory is stored in the Hippocampus—which grows new brain cells throughout our life and is the area of the brain responsible for processing and retrieving information. It is adversely affected by the hormone Cortisol which is produced in response to prolonged stress; and it is the first area to be affected by Alzheimer's disease. Long-term memories are 'stored' in various 'association cortices', or files, in the brain.

We can all have memory lapses too. Yesterday I was cleaning my house, which is an 'automatic' task; and I was thinking of other things whilst doing this work. I suddenly realised that I couldn't be sure what and where I'd cleaned 'because my mind was elsewhere'. I doubt that would be a good defence for shoplifting but I can understand how it happens if we are pre-occupied or mentally distracted and 'forget' what we're doing.

The bad news is that our memory function declines with age—according to recent research. This ten-year study has revealed that our ability to remember everyday things starts to decline from the age of 45 years; with both men and women suffering the same 3.6% loss in memory power between the ages of 45 and 49 years. Other studies have shown that we all seem to suffer some loss of mental processing speed from the age of 20 years!

For most of us though the problem is with retrieval rather than storage of our memories. Much of what we learn gets misplaced rather than actually lost. Our overall 'memory power' drops because as we age, the levels of neurotransmitters in the brain decline. This decrease in 'brain chemicals' causes us to become more easily distracted too.

Now, where was I? Oh yes, I remember.....there is some good news too! A bit of stress can be good for the brain and keep it stimulated and efficient. Our brain also has 'neural-plasticity', whereby it can repair and reconfigure itself and add new connections (called Neuro-genesis) in order to cope with demand. As we age, the two sides, or hemispheres, of our brain work better together which allows us to 'see the bigger picture' and think more broadly. New research also shows that we can continue to grow Myelin in our brain well into late middle-age. This fatty coating covers and protects the neurons and makes connections between them more effective. So we become 'wiser with age' as we accumulate knowledge and can 'network' this around the brain.

The old adage 'use it or lose it' is still true. Learning new things allows us to continue to learn new things ......remember that!

Sleep Problems? Tired of Feeling Tired?

The quality of your sleep greatly affects all areas of your life. There are millions of people who are sleep-deprived....which may be good news for the pharmaceutical companies but not for the body, mind and soul of those insomniacs!

Your body both repairs itself and processes the day's experiences during sleep. In previous generations people had 8-9 hours sleep, whereas nowadays many people report having only 5-7 hours of sleep. The quality of your sleep is vital. Brief naps can help you to recharge your batteries in the mid-afternoon, but at night time we should be following our body clock (circadian rhythms) and allowing the Melatonin we produce—from our stocks of Serotonin—to guide us into the Delta brainwave frequency necessary for sleep.

We have different cycles within our overall sleep cycle every night—the main ones being Rapid Eye Movement sleep—when we dream and our body should be inert to avoid us acting out our dreams—and the deeper restorative sleep we need to rebalance our complex body chemistry.

Stress and lack of sleep play havoc with our bodies—resulting in less Myelin laid down on nerve cells, which mean that we cannot think properly and are likely to have neurological problems too. Extreme sleep deprivation leads to psychosis—which is why it has been used as a method of torture!

According to Professor Colin Espie of the University of Glasgow, Scotland, (who has studied the sleep patterns of 12,000 adults) 51% of adults struggle to get to sleep and remain asleep; and of these 75% were women and 25% men. There may be many contributory factors to this imbalance such as women's tendency to over-worry, and men's physically demanding jobs, amongst other possible causes. As a result of a lack of good sleep 55% reported relationship problems; 77% were affected by lack of concentration; 64% said that they were less productive at work; 83% had mood problems and 93% lacked energy. So there are far reaching problems in the working and personal lives of many people. Getting enough sleep can mean the difference between a sick, tired, foggy and unfocussed life; and one in which you are healthy, alert, effective and productive.

Moderate and long-term sleep deprivation leads to increased Cortisol levels (implicated in depression and death of brain cells in the memory and mood centres of the brain called the Hippocampus); increased insulin levels; weight gain; increases in the hormone Grehlin which increases hunger and also lowers your appetite suppressing hormone known as PYY. You will eat more to compensate for the lack of sleep and you will crave more sugars, refined carbohydrates and stimulants as a result. Sleep deprivation can also lead to depression, attention-deficit-disorder, problems with learning and memory; as well as being a contributing factor to more severe health conditions.

Stress, worry, fear and anxiety can create a vicious circle when we are trying to go to sleep. We can be plagued by the mind-chatter or head-heckling that prevents us from shifting-gear down to Theta brainwave activity and then into the Delta brainwave state associated with sleep. WE CANNOT THINK AND SLEEP AT THE SAME TIME—but switching off our 'thinking' requires focussed effort.

General 'advice' from magazines tells us to do what, for many of us, is obvious—such as not having caffeine drinks before bed-time, staying cool, being in a darkened room in a comfortable bed and without electronic gadgets close by, and having scented candles and a warm bath with essential oils such as lavender. These will all help, but they still don't address the real issue for many people. What they fail to tell us is that unless your brainwaves are slowed down to a Delta wave frequency—which is between 1-4 cycles per second—you will not be able to sleep. The 'thinking/worrying/planning' state of mind is associated with Beta brainwave frequencies which are much faster at between 13-30 cycles per second.

Experiencing extreme exhaustion may be necessary for some people to finally be able to stop responding to the barrage of thoughts, images and ideas generated by an area of the brain called the Reticular Activating System. This is repeatedly bringing random and trivial thoughts to our awareness; and we then pick up on these and go off on a 'what-if' or 'will I be good enough?' etc. mental dialogue—until we learn how to observe this process and put a stop to it. We can then allow ourselves to slip down into the calmer, slower 'zone' necessary for sleep.

Brainwave entrainment has been shown to greatly improve sleep as well as dealing with the troublesome anxieties and fears that keep our minds churning instead of allowing them to slow down.

There are specific ways to get our body/mind into a sleep state—but they do require practice—sometimes several times before you will get into the Delta brainwave state.

I have created a simple method for this. I call it a 'BEER for bedtime'! BEER is an acronym for the four stages required, and, in simple abridged terms, these relate to slowing down the Breath, lowering the Eyes (which will keep rising as you begin 'thinking' again so you will need to persevere); Emptying the mind and Relaxing the body....all of which prepare your body for sleep.

Taking nutritional supplements such as GABA and Melatonin (both of which are available via the internet as they are not on general retail sale in UK) as well as 5HTP—which is a precursor to Serotonin and Melatonin—will all help; and Magnesium is known to be beneficial in calming the body, particularly if we are fidgety and restless.

None of these have the 'side effects' associated with pharmaceutical drugs such as Zopiclone, Zalepon and Zolpidem—which include loss of taste, nausea, vomiting, dry mouth, dizziness and drowsiness, headache, diarrhoea, and hallucinations. Withdrawal from these prescribed drugs can actually bring about insomnia, anxiety, tremor, loss of appetite, perspiration and tinnitus! These drugs are also potentially addictive!

IT'S A NO BRAINER...... SLEEP WELL, AND LIVE WELL!

Needy or Greedy?

Greed is in the news ......again!

We regularly hear and see reports about the greed of looters, and benefit cheats, and the greed of the corporate and banking executives. So is it just a human trait that we should expect to see? Maybe it is just a sin that we are all potentially guilty of?

The underlying motive and reason for greed can be—at its most basic level—survival; as seen in the greed of the starving homeless in third world countries when food and blanket deliveries arrive. The 'me-first' attitude is then easy to understand. Even the recent looting—linked to civil unrest and rioting—made some sense in view of the 'emotional contagion' and shared sense of greed that was around. Benefit cheats may feel that they are not depriving another 'person' of money—simply taking more than they should from a government purse; and as such their sense of 'guilt and shame' is diminished. It is harder to understand the greed of the wealthy. In such cases there seems to be a personal belief that 'I must get as much as I possibly can—and as much as I can get away with before I am judged, held accountable, or rejected by others, for my greed.'

There is a huge waste of money, resources and energy in our society, and we have learned to desensitize ourselves to this. We have also learned not to trust the powerful 'decision-makers' who determine the conditions of our lives. Fear of having to rely upon an unreliable provider, and the fear of going without, of missing out, or of other people having something instead of me having it, all fuel selfishness and greed.

There is, however, a level of selfishness that is good, healthy and appropriate. We need to 'breath-in from the oxygen mask' to enable us to then help those alongside us who are more vulnerable. To take care of ourselves so that we can then in turn be able to take care of others. We should value and respect ourselves and our needs, and strive to get these reasonably met as best we can—but not at the cost of someone else's quality and experience of life.

Many of us grew up in a sibling group where we learned to be greedy because it was wise to get as much food as we could, and if possible to go back for seconds—or even thirds in my case when it came to school dinners! I still 'regress' to being greedy after a big meal or at a dinner party—if there are chocolates and desserts to be had!

In therapy, if a client acknowledges their greed and any difficulties this has brought to them and their partner and family, we can then look at the underlying fear and dread that 'not-having' brings to them. They may have been a 'hoarder'—saving up food or objects as a defence against 'famine' and poverty, to ensure their survival in the event of their worst-case-scenario. They may have an underlying fear that no-one will help or support them if they should ever need it, and that they must be overly independent and 'look after number one.'

It is understandable that we want to improve our own lives, and the opportunities and quality of life for members of our families. It makes sense to aspire to become better and to receive the appropriate rewards for our efforts. But the present rampant greed exhibited by the already wealthy few in our society shows a frightening trend of ignorance, disregard, and blindness to the loss of fairness and proportionality. Only this week an oil painting was sold for £160 million pounds! No doubt there will now have to be great expense incurred in protecting this 'treasure' from theft!

I am not politically-minded and probably never will be; but I do believe that we all deserve the same chances, and that we can then make of these what we will. These fair chances and opportunities are greatly reduced by the diminishing amount of money available to meet the needs of the members of society. The 'money-pot' is massively depleted by greed, selfishness and thoughtless waste. The fears and selfishness of those who can 'get-away-with-it' in the corporate banking and finance world have a very negative effect upon those lower-down the pecking order.

We know from Abraham Maslow's 'Heirarchy of Needs Pyramid,' created decades ago, that we all still share the same basic needs—shown at the bottom of his pyramid—such as shelter, food, clothing and care; and that as we have our needs met at one level, then our higher needs emerge waiting to be met. Too many people cannot afford homes, or to heat their homes. They cannot afford to eat well or to maintain their health. They cannot afford life-saving medications, they cannot afford necessary medical and nursing care or medical operations. So much is being 'skimmed-off' by those who have the know-how and selfish, greedy motives; and so much is just wasted on 'moth-balled' projects, 'professional consultants', and many other short-sighted and fruitless ventures. Greed depletes the 'pot' that should provide for more people to rise higher up that pyramid and live more fruitful and enhanced lives. Greed must be held in check, if not by ourselves, then by powerful social influences and conditions. Sadly those in power have often been shown to lack such incentive or desire to rein-in their greed.... and it grows greater as the Haves and Have-nots become further and further apart. Greed of the few has to be paid for by the many.

If you become aware of greed in your own life, and in the lives of those around you, then perhaps you will be intrigued enough to question its presence and purpose. To have a little more than we need helps us to feel a bit more secure in an insecure world, and buffers us from any acute shocks that might befall us. It is when this excess over requirements starts to build up that we really need to question whether greed is hiding an underlying fear or dread; and if so, what other, fairer and more compassionate ways there might be of soothing these fears, that don't involve the acquisition of more and more 'stuff' or money—both of which ultimately become a daily burden and liability that drains your energy as you are compelled to give it your attention.

Meeting your own real needs is necessary and admirable; whereas being greedy is not.

S.O.S. ....WE ARE AWASH WITH ANXIETY!

Many of us are struggling to keep our heads above the water long enough to take a good deep breath. The 'daily news' keeps rocking our boat by evoking fear and anxiety. The waters are made choppy and the boat we're rowing is letting in water. We may have had an oar snatched away from us and no matter how hard we keep rowing we are getting nowhere, and only going around in circles. We are not alone—so many others are also 'hyper-aroused' and struggling to make progress. We all affect one another by our moods and behaviours and so anxiety 'ripples' on and on.

This heightened emotional state we call Anxiety has a detrimental effect upon all of our body systems; our ability to think and plan; our sleep patterns; our ability to fight off infections and heal our wounds; our relationships.... in fact our whole lives! Certain parts of the brain are over-working—which has a knock-on effect too, and this, especially if combined with lack of sleep, results in a form of Depression.

All that we used to be able to 'rely-upon' can suddenly become unpredictable and transient. Our work contracts; our home and its monetary value; or planning for our old-age.... is all in a state of flux. Previous generations had different types of stress to those of the present day, but stress, anxiety and fear all erode the basis of our lives. Our brains can't tell the difference between a real physical threat to our lives, and the feelings created by the hormones adrenalin and cortisol that we produce in response to the ongoing scaremongering media 'news', combined with our active imaginations. At our baseline and primitive level we still activate the vitally important questions "will I survive....will I belong....will I thrive?"

Too many of us nowadays are struggling and worrying about keeping our homes, having enough food to eat, and keeping warm and safe. We become focussed upon these basic human needs and cannot give any energy to our other 'higher' needs such as learning new things and appreciating the beauty of each new moment.

Our anxiety can take many forms such as obsessions and compulsions, social and performance anxiety or even a free flowing general anxiety. We are struggling to feel safe in an unsafe world. So...that's the reality for most of us....but what can we do about it?

We cannot simply 'think' our way out of a heightened emotional state, neither can we rely upon affirmations and prayers. The only way to reduce your anxiety levels at the outset is to change your physiology. The first step is with the breath. Slowing down your breathing and extending the outgoing breath activates the parasympathetic nervous system which is our natural 'soother'. Slowing down the breath is as easy as breathing in to the silent count of eight (or less if that is too many for you), and then slowly breathing out to the count of 12 (or less if needs be—as long as the number is at least four counts higher than the incoming breath was). Do this at least four times. When we have calmed down the breath and released the tension in our bodies we can then refocus our attention and awareness and give our brain a reprieve from the incessant ruminating on things, and the draining mind-chatter/head-heckling that we do to ourselves. We can take back control of our cognitive abilities and reclaim our 'common sense', rational perspective, and our ability to find a solution that fits for us.

Personally, I also master any anxiety by making sure that I eat well, with proteins included in most meals. I eat simple, natural and inexpensive food, and I top-up with some natural supplements, which include an all-round vitamin and mineral mixture, B-complex vitamins, Omega 3 fish oils and magnesium, to give my body the full range of nutrients it needs to make the vital chemicals, enzymes, hormones, and neurotransmitters necessary for good functioning. Having my blood-sugar levels balanced also helps to soothe certain anxious feelings which can result from the pancreas being put under erratic pressure when dealing with fluctuating levels of sugar in the bloodstream. I also listen to specific sounds that harmonize with my brain and bring it into a relaxed state—called Brainwave Entrainment (see www.qpp.uk.com for more information about this). This also ensures that I sleep well and thereby give my brain a few hours to recuperate and to produce the feel-good chemicals that further help to keep anxiety at bay.

The body produces its own natural 'tranquiliser' in the form of GABA (GammaAminoButyricAcid), but these levels can be depleted by inadequate diet, lack of good sleep, and ongoing stress. It can be purchased over the internet (as it is no longer available in retail stores in the UK). I personally find that GABA leaves me too calm and chilled out, but I know some people who find it very helpful.

"If the situation or problem is such that it can be remedied, then there is no need to worry about it; alternatively, if there is no way out, no solution, no possibility of resolution, then there is also no point in being worried about it, because you can't do anything about it anyway".....HH Dalai Lama

Are You Fed-Up with Feeling Fed-Up?

The recent news of a sport personality's suicide has aroused surprise, and many questions..... "Why would someone with apparently so much to live for decide to end their life?".... "If he couldn't cope with the difficulties of life then what chance is there for the rest of us who don't have anything like the great life that he had?"

There are many ways to commit suicide, and many reasons for it too. Some people who have survived have said that they wanted to 'kill off' a part of themselves; perhaps, for instance, the public persona which had to endure the shame and humiliation of the exposure of acts of 'wrong-doing'. We find it easier to understand suicide when it is used to end the pain and suffering of terminal illness; or following the death of a loved one. It requires planning and preparation and is not usually carried out by people who are in the grip of a deep depression.

Depression is a word used to describe a whole spectrum of emotional states—from being low/flat/unfulfilled/thwarted in our life, right through to the inability to get out of bed in the morning and face another day. A medical diagnosis of depression usually results in a prescription for pharmaceutical drugs—which have been shown to have very limited benefits and several unpleasant side effects. These drugs attempt to treat the symptoms and not the causes—which could be either internal or external.

There are physical causes for a depressed mood too—such as low-thyroid functioning, parasites, candida, hormonal or blood sugar imbalances, food sensitivities, post-natal, dehydration, and nutritional deficiencies. These will need to be checked out and rectified by a qualified naturopath who uses an holistic and natural approach to health care.

We may have a genetic 'predisposition' to low moods; and if this is followed by negative life experiences we are much more likely to live with the dark heavy cloud of depression hanging around us.

Depression manifests itself in a variety of ways, and understanding these can be of help by itself, as the cognitive part of the brain is able to 'make sense' of the mood disorder. This takes some of the pressure off the emotional part of the brain. Excessive activity in the Basal Ganglia region of the emotional part of our brain—due to prolonged anxiety—can result in the Deep Limbic area of the brain in turn becoming affected. This leads to depression and the associated imbalance of mood-enhancing chemicals (neurotransmitters).

Anxiety, fear, and ruminating about our worries affects both our sleep cycle and its quality. Without our regular full quota of deep restorative sleep we can become 'depressed' and lacking in energy and vitality.

We often think that someone with depression has an under-working brain but in fact the opposite is usually the case—it can result from an over-active brain that needs to 'tune-out' and take time to withdraw, in order to salvage and preserve its depleted energy resources. Hence the difficulty with starting exercise—which is known to help the condition—we just cannot spare the energy!

There are natural remedies that really help depression including Magnesium, B-vitamins, Omega 3's, SAMe, 5HTP (from the amino acid L-Tryptophan which creates more Serotonin and thereby raises the mood). For some people St John's Wort can be helpful—but check for any incompatibility with other medications/birth-control pills.

Our Negative Inner Self Talk, and Automatic Negative Thoughts, can hold us in a cycle of negative thinking and the associated bodily responses; and we 'do' depression with our body posture and facial expressions too! These are more complex and broader causes which are outside the scope of this article, but they are well covered by 'The Ripple Effect' Process.

At a deeper level you may have a sub-conscious belief system that holds you in a depressed, hopeless and helpless place in your life. This belief system is 'running the show' of our lives over 90% of the time and cannot be changed by drugs or talking therapies alone.

Conventional talking therapies cannot change this deeper 'script' or change the associated unhelpful and obsolete 'programming' that we may still be carrying with us from childhood, and which still holds us in its grip.

First of all we must find out if our depressed mood has a physical or an emotional/psychological cause. We can reflect upon the role it plays in our life and whether we are committed to removing it or at least greatly reducing it. Then comes the unearthing of the conditions which have allowed it to flourish until now; and finally the treatment needed to bring about a change in focus to a life that isn't 'drowning in depression'—but one which allows us to keep our heads above water and be able to see the wider, brighter vista with optimism and hope.

Anger—Friend or Foe?

What is your immediate bodily response to reading the word 'anger'?

Your thoughts and feelings about it stem from your own personal experiences of anger, and what you have heard or read about it. We see anger exist in a wide spectrum of behaviours, from an irritated person's foot/finger-tapping—right through to violent and destructive rage where people and/or property are damaged.

We frequently see television coverage of civil unrest and violent struggles for democracy; the outrage at the exploitation of, and cruelty towards, vulnerable children, the elderly, the sick, and animals; the threat to our livelihoods caused by Government policy changes—which we then also feel impotent to challenge effectively, and this fuels our anger even further.

We can become 'de-sensitised' to all of the anger we witness—but we are still emotionally and psychologically affected by it. Perhaps it triggers memories of an angry household that we grew up in, or what we experienced of anger in school; or of a 'rage' incident we have been a part of; or of gang violence; or the violent public disorders seen over the decades of our lives.

We may have been 'conditioned' in childhood not to allow ourselves to feel, let alone to express, anger. Instead it festers within us, affecting our physical and emotional/psychological health. We may have had to develop a 'mask' to wear, instead of being authentic and showing our real emotions.

Alternatively we may have learned to scare people with our anger and to get own way. Our anger may be a cover up for our deeper sadness, sorrow and despair that we won't allow ourselves to feel, because we fear it will be too overwhelming. Instead we show the world our 'angry and aggressive self', whose deeper purpose is to protect our own vulnerability from further pain.

Some people will evoke and invite an angry response from others—and then pretend that they have no idea why people react to them with hostility. These are the people that are always late, forgetful, play the 'victim that no-one can rescue', create disharmony with their malicious gossip etc. They create anger around them but they don't accept responsibility for doing so.

If we are afraid or ashamed of our own anger we will probably stuff it down or 'divert' or 'displace' it into certain behaviours. These behaviours can range from some forms of self-harm to lashing out at inanimate objects. If we don't learn how to express our anger in a healthy way, we store it up and it can instead flood out as if a dam had burst—usually in a situation that doesn't warrant anything like the level of anger we are showing.

When we are angry, or furious, we cannot think clearly and we cannot express ourselves clearly or effectively. We will probably be shouting as an attempt to gain the upper-hand, and we look aggressive and threatening to others. This in turn activates something in them, based upon their own history and relationship with anger and what it has led to in their own past.

We often 're-play' in our mind angry scenarios and think about what we wished we'd said and done, which can then further increase feelings of frustration and disappointment in ourselves. A healthier scenario is to develop the calm assertive language of the Sensible

Adult in you—and to express your level of anger at the right person, in the right way and at the right time. We need to learn how to understand and control our emotions, and then to choose to respond to a situation assertively, rather than just emotionally reacting to things around us like an angry child would do.

Bear in mind that every thought you have affects every cell in your body—and that we can become 'addicted' to the frequent cascade of chemicals within our bodies which result from our frequent thoughts, and the situations we attract to ourselves. A negative loop begins—made worse by the 'negative filter' we then create which ensures that we then perceive new events with the contamination of our old experiences. We all literally 'project' our meaning onto an event or person and react/behave 'as-if' it were the truth! Self-fulfilling prophesies do exist!

Our emotions affect those around us and in turn we are affected by those people that we are around, which is called 'Emotional Contagion'. You have to decide who you want to spend your time with based upon the extent to which they enhance your sense of well-being—or not.

If anger has too big a part in your life, and causes you and those around you problems, then it is your responsibility to master it and change it into your ally rather than your enemy. By diffusing the powerful part that anger has played in your life you will be free to choose a more balanced and calm way of responding, rather than just reacting emotionally to a person or situation which, on reflection, probably wasn't worth the turmoil of you getting so upset anyway. We all get angry, it is just a matter of turning it into something useful and empowering, and not being held captive by it and allowing anger to damage your relationships or career.

Anger can however be a good thing. It can energise us to protect our personal and family boundaries, to keep ourselves, and those we care about, safe from harm. It can give us the courage to challenge threats to our integrity and well-being. In this respect anger is a helpful emotion and our friend rather than our foe.

KEEP CALM AND CARRY ON!

Well—that *sounds* easy enough!

Our brain is not a fixed and solid entity; it is always in a state of change….in fact you are almost entirely made up of empty space, with a few chemical and electrical reactions taking place in between. Changing the way your brain works is therefore possible, and is usually necessary.

When we are emotionally aroused by anxiety, fear, anger and distress we are operating from the emotional—or Limbic—part of our brain; and we cannot then accurately perceive events, see our options, or the consequences of our behaviour. Neither can we think or express ourselves clearly. We are stuck in Fight-Flight-Freeze-Flop mode—which is our more primitive way of reacting to difficulties.

To be able to 'calm down and think straight' we must begin with calming and soothing the body; then shifting our focus of awareness; and then we can examine and change our thought processes. Changing how we breathe (by slowing down and deepening the in-breath and extending the out-breath, and by using several additional techniques too if needs be) is the first and only natural way to begin to soothe and calm ourselves down. We are then slowing down our heart-rate and turning down the adrenalin response.

We can also learn how to shift our awareness to 'inside', and to the present moment. From that place—in the 'here and now' of our lives—we can then rebalance and understand our emotions, thoughts and mental images, and to take back control of them.

Our brain notices a massive amount of information every second—far too much for us to consciously register. We can choose to focus our attention onto some of this data about our present moment experience—for instance, by becoming an 'observer of the detail' of aspects of our environment—and thereby take our attention *away from* our usual focus upon the past or future. We tend to spend too much time worrying about an imaginary future scenario, or in replaying the past which can't be changed.

We can only be happy if we can calm our minds and control our thoughts. We can then choose, and allow, the thoughts that actually serve us well—and throw out those that don't. Those to be discarded may well be the majority of our usual thoughts such as our habitual thinking about 'Trivia' (thoughts that are somehow related to our lives but are not really relevant or helpful) and 'Trash' (thoughts that are random, and unrelated).

The fast-and-cheap Cognitive Behavioural Therapy favoured by the NHS has only limited effectiveness. You are so much more than just your thoughts—and you cannot change your thoughts until you have learned how to soothe your physical and emotional states first. This is particularly so if your anxiety/terror originates from a physical and potentially life-threatening event such as a severe illness or a near-death experience which results in your emotional brain being on hyper-alert for further threats. The Limbic/emotional brain needs to feel 'safe' and 'soothed' again before any further therapeutic work can begin.

We have a part of our brain called the Reticular Activating System which randomly fires out thoughts and ideas for us to pick up on and ruminate over. When we wake up too early it is this area of the brain that kicks-in and fills our head with 'thoughts' that we don't want to be having. Another part of the brain, called the Cingulate region, can keep us stuck in over-thinking about things too.

Your thoughts cause your suffering—and you can choose to change them. You get what you think about. Do you want to give permission for negative thoughts to stay around and to drain your energy?

So, in a nutshell, in order to calm down and think straight we must first calm and soothe our bodies and then we can re-balance our minds. We can find out about, and understand, the causes and history of our distress, and train ourselves to become 'mindful' of what we are experiencing and thinking, and why.

Those all important enemies—the Negative Inner Self Talk and Automatic Negative Thoughts that are running our lives from the shadows, need to be examined and challenged, changed and controlled, so that they cannot continue to agitate us, or sabotage our well-being, or scupper our attempts at regulating our emotions. Psycho-Emotional-Education will help with all of these areas and bring about lasting change that enables you to keep calm and carry on.

Your 'Inner-Child'

You may have heard this term and thought it was just another bit of 'psycho-babble'; even though the term has been around for many years now. Your Inner Child is the echo of the child you once were.

We each have our own history and we have all been influenced by our environment, events and the significant people around us. Up to the age of six years, our brain was functioning at a relatively slow pace—Theta brainwave frequency—which is a very 'receptive' brainwave state—and we would have been profoundly affected by our experiences. We will have made 'decisions' at a sub-conscious level, about how we 'should' be and what we 'should' do in order to be seen as OK, and to be allowed to stay around and to 'survive' in our families.

Our later experiences will have reinforced these beliefs and formed our own 'Script' for how our life 'should' be. We carry these immature scripts and decisions with us into adulthood—when they run our lives more than 90% of the time. It therefore makes sense that we should revisit the experiences of the child we once were, and to find out what our own script says about our life and the unfolding drama we have been creating. Not doing so will result in our playing out of the same unexamined script and drama over and over again. We cannot change the script by talking about it, or by conscious effort alone. It was designed to keep us safe—albeit in ways that now hinder us—and so it isn't given up that easily!

Most of the time we are living life like a child inside a 'grown-up' body; and the 'child' within us yearns for help, care and understanding. We may try to silence these deeper longings by using alcohol or drugs, by promiscuity, gambling, over-spending, over-eating, work-aholism, self-harming and other ways of avoiding the real and deeper needs we have. Needs which we haven't allowed ourselves to become fully aware of, or to find a way to have sufficiently met.

We have all been influenced by our environments since the time we were in our mothers' wombs. The sounds around us, our mothers' stress levels, the abundance or deficit of the 'feel-good' hormones and neuro-peptides, the nourishment or lack of it, complications, twin-pregnancies, drugs, alcohol, and infections will all have played their part in how safe we felt even before we were born.

Then the actual birth experience, and our early infant care and the 'emotional availability' of our mother will have either reinforced or soothed those earlier influences. As small children we will have been absorbing a great deal from our extended families, our caregiver(s), friends, pre-school and early school years, and religious institutions. We may not have had words for these experiences but they will have been 'logged' in our sub-conscious minds and bodies.

This all creates the pool in which we float, or sink. Inevitably, the water will be dirty and murky—or it may even be like thick mud. In this pool resides our self-esteem, body-image, family trauma, shame and secrets (even if not spoken about—as they all affect the quality of the care our caregivers are able to show to us.) We will sink down into this pool, or mud, when we are overwhelmed by our thoughts, emotions, self-doubt or self-loathing.

In therapy an aim should be to sensitively lift out this mud, bit by bit, until we are left with just a stain. We must also learn how not to 'top-it-up' with more mud—either by doing it ourselves, or by being around other people who want to dump some of their own 'mud' onto us instead of dealing with it, and cleaning it up, themselves.

Signs that your Inner Child is wounded will be shown in: low self-esteem; poor body-image; mood and emotional imbalances; problems with boundaries being too rigid or too weak; problems with eating; harming yourself; psycho-sexual difficulties; being 'false' and wearing 'masks'; identity problems; being a rebel, a hoarder, a bully, a perennial victim or a super-achiever; intimacy problems; commitment problems; a general lack of trust in yourself and others; criminal behaviour; excessive lying; being 'overly-responsible' for others; being fiercely competitive and a poor loser; dependencies and addictions; lack of friends; obsessive and needy behaviour; fear of authority figures; being manipulative; being passive, or being aggressive.

That's a long—and sadly not exhaustive—list. It is the stuff that brings people into psychotherapy. To repair and heal the wounds caused by parents, and others, who didn't know any better. It is always about the unmet needs of the Inner Child!

We can learn how to meet, rescue and 'adopt' this wounded child who still lives deep inside us. After all, you are the only person who you can guarantee never to leave you!

We can each learn too how to revise our sub-conscious belief system and write a new and improved script for the rest of our own life-drama. We can then ring-fence and emotionally contain and soothe our Inner Child, and allow the Competent Adult inside us to 'attend to business' out in the world. However, we must regularly keep in touch with what our Inner Child still needs from us—which is, to be truly cared for by someone who wants the very best for them—you!

If you have a photograph of yourself as a small child, this will help you to reconnect with him/her—the aim of which is to now understand their plight and to show them/yourself the compassion that has been missing. It is often easier to feel compassion for other people than it is for yourself and you may have been rejecting and ignoring the yearning of your Inner Child who has been calling out to you, over many years, for your interest, attention, compassion and love. It may mean you now allowing yourself to have 'treats' and rewards that you would never have allowed yourself, or have been allowed by your parents, in the past. The sensible competent Adult part of you should be able to set fair and sensible boundaries around this, so that you do not over-indulge yourself or use rewards as either a distraction or as a cover up for your deeper pain.

If you have difficulties accessing this Adult part of your inner psyche then psychotherapy will be of help to you, providing that it includes this aspect of integrating the hidden or lost aspects of your character and personality, to help you on your path to becoming a more well-rounded and complete person.

Rescuing and re-parenting your Inner Child will allow you to 'fill in the gaps' and enable you to live a more positive and rewarding life—with fun, laughter, spontaneity, authenticity, and most importantly, with love.

Split Personality

I am not talking here about Multiple Personality Disorder (otherwise called Dissociative Identity Disorder), or Schizophrenia. I refer instead to the parts of us that have become 'split-off' as a result of our childhood experiences, and the meaning we gave to these from our under-developed child-brain.

There are two levels of splitting that take place when we believe that we are 'not good enough' as we are. The first level happens as we learn that in order to be seen as OK and to be accepted within the family, we have to 'wear a mask', and fulfil the 'role' set for us by our own family. These masks might include the 'smiley-face-everything-is-fine-in-our family' mask; the 'I-feel-no-pain' mask; and the 'I-must-be-a-good boy/girl-at-all-times-and-not-be-a-burden' mask.

We may also have a 'role' to play in the family unit such as the Super-achiever, the Caretaker, the Carrier of the family madness/badness, the Sick Patient, and many more besides. All of these rob us of our authenticity and the belief that we are OK just as we are; and we don't feel wanted or valued for simply being our **real self**. Instead we develop a **false-self** to please other people and to ensure that we can continue to live with them and to have our basic survival needs met by them.

For too many people these 'masks' become stuck and they forget they are even wearing them; or they fear ever taking off the mask and having to face, and live with, the stranger who lies beneath; or they may have tried and failed to remove the mask which then stays in place because of pressure from other people who want/need them to keep wearing it!

A second and deeper split occurs as a result of severe childhood trauma, abuse and abandonment; when the real self, hidden behind the false self, steps or falls back even further ....from the back-room and down into the cellar. Often to be banished and forgotten about, this 'prisoner' is condemned to a life of darkness and the struggle to survive emotionally. It lives in shame of its own existence. It feels like an alien without a true personality or life of its own. It becomes the puppet for others to use, whether that be within the family, or with partners later in their life and within their inevitably dysfunctional relationships. 'It' observes the unfolding 'drama' of life as if from a distance, without any feeling of deeper connection to life. It is isolated and hopeless. It feels like an 'it'. Believing itself to be deeply flawed and feeling the intense pain of rejection, ridicule and hostility, it knows only self-loathing and despair. Any words of encouragement, care, or concern echo around the dank cellar in which it exists. Nothing good can penetrate—the fear of further wounding is so great. Exposure and shame burn like a branding iron telling all of its failure as a human being. It abides in a prison cell of its own making, which is actually locked from the inside, or the door may be ajar but the prisoner dare not try to escape. The dark damp cell is at least a familiar 'home'.

Maybe you have tried—in vain—to have a relationship with what I am calling a **'Cellar Dweller'**? You may have poured considerable effort and time into trying to coax them out and to help them to believe in your honesty and integrity....but to no avail. Maybe you have got as far as marriage to such a lost soul—who went along with the arrangement in order to have some 'comfort' pushed through the bars of their inner prison. If so, you will get little in return as they won't know how to love, let alone how to show it in a way that reaches another's soul. They may receive your love but not know how to give back anything meaningful of themselves. They may talk at length without really saying anything about themselves or their innermost dreams, hopes, and needs.....because they are detached from these and unable and unwilling to take the risk of possible rejection by anyone else. They have already profoundly rejected themselves.

It seems all too obvious to the rest of us that they should simply realise that they are now an adult, and that they can change their thought processes, and consequently their feelings and behaviours. However their detachment from life and their self-loathing is so deeply ingrained that any such wise words would be wasted on them. They could not penetrate their protective armour.

They may fear the prospect of living and dying alone, and so form an 'entanglement' with someone—rather than a real relationship. Very few people would settle for the meagre offerings that the Cellar Dweller might bring to a relationship....perhaps only another deeply wounded soul would accept the profound lack of emotional expression and intimacy. Cellar dwellers usually find another cellar dweller to have a type of 'mutually dependant' relationship with, devoid of real depth, intimacy or passion. They become companions from adjoining cells and they pretend that the bars are not a barrier, but of course they are. So, outwardly such a couple may appear to 'function' well, and may even have professional jobs, and some social status. But a 'fly-on-the-wall' would witness two aliens living like magnets emotionally repelling one another, and moving around without actually touching.

Shame is called the master emotion—for its power to disintegrate our sense of Self. Shame creates the prison in which the 'unworthy' reside. Only by shining a light of loving compassion which illuminates the dark recesses and takes away the heavy shadows can an imprisoned soul be gently coaxed to come to the edge of their sanctuary/prison in the cellar of their life, and step out towards the light. Like a terrified kitten who dreads the next kick, many will not take that risk and instead they will continue to play safe or play dead, whilst still trying so hard to fool others, and themselves, into believing that they are 'fine'.

I have written a few poems to share with you now which speak from this lonely prison of the 'cellar dweller'—the hidden part of the psyche that hides where eyes cannot see and happiness doesn't reach. These are written both from my own experiences and from glimpses I have had into the darkness of other people's inner sanctuary, their fears, despair and hopes.

Words from the Unseen Place

Where the Heart Hides Waiting

Waiting

I hide deep in the shadows of my own soul
A prisoner with a key that doesn't fit the lock
Subdued and resigned to my solitary fate
I wait, pale and thin, weak and dirty

Neglected and abandoned
The cold darkness is my only companion
A few scraps of hope my only nourishment
I yearn for the warmth of the sun

The distant cries of seagulls mock my fate as they fly free
And children's laughter stabs my heart
As I wait to be allowed to play too
I hide my despair and pretend I don't care

Not daring to dream of seeing the eyes of love
Or feeling safe in the arms of a rescuer
I am lost and forgotten
But still I wait....I wait...

Despair

I am like a chameleon who blends into your life
And I find somewhere to belong, for a while
I only show you what I can bear you to see
But I dare not show you Me

So no-one really sees me or even knows I am here
I am even becoming invisible to myself
The aching to be wanted engulfs me
Yet the fear of exposure paralyses me

If my searching eyes should one day hold your gaze
My heart may yield despite its pain
And my tears of relief may flow at last
As our eyes and souls meet.

I know that my time is running out
Please find me and end my despair.

Why Not Me?

If life was fair then mine would be vibrant too
Instead I must silently watch
Whilst others receive all I wish I could have
I dare not hope for my dreams to come true

What did I do so wrong to have been branded a burden
Hated and beaten
In my loneliness I feel the shame
Of the past I did and didn't have

I try to be like the lucky ones
And act as if I was loved too
I pretend to myself that my wounds aren't there
But they gape and bleed, raw and sore

Whatever I try to heal them with fails
No soothing comes
Nothing can replace the lack of a parent's love
It's not fair.....will it ever be my turn?

Facade

My facade will fool you
I've created it that way
So you will think me normal
And worthy of your time

On the stage of my life
You will believe the carefully painted set to be solid
But you do not see the flimsy wooden framework
Trying so hard to hold it all in place

It could collapse at any time
And I would be exposed to a disappointed audience
No applause for me, just derision and ridicule
As everything is sucked away in the tornado of my shame

So I must struggle each day
To keep the facade in place
And convince you that it's real
So that you will want me here.

Rescue

I have found the emotional orphan
And carefully released her from your grip
She longed for discovery and freedom
But could not believe it would ever come

Her sensitive emotional antennae
Scanned for even a hint of impending pain
Fearing the fate of the miner's canary
When exposed to toxic gas

You gave her a fist instead of a hug
A kick instead of a smile
Ridicule instead of interest
Shame instead of love.

Telling her it was for her own good
When it never could have been
Your belated tearful apology didn't heal the wounds
It came much too late for that

Now I have her and she is safe with me
I will soothe her wounded soul
And teach her how to forgive your ignorance
As she learns how to fly free at last.

Psyche Bites

The following 'short and sweet' mini articles will, I hope, give you a little more to think about.

Love is the Drug

Our brains are already 'hard-wired' to experience joy, bliss and serenity; and yet so many people look outside of themselves for this 'buzz'; in the form of alcohol, drugs, mood-enhancing addictions and dysfunctional/dramatic/exciting/risky relationships.

Love is called the 'universal energy' as it unites us and raises our spiritual energy.

There are different types of love, some of which will give us our 'natural high' and others that deplete our energy.

* Mature love = I need you because I love you
* Immature love = I love you because I need you

Types of Love

* Eros—Romantic love, beauty, perfection and sensuality.
* Ludos—Game-playing love, with lots of flirtation, but a lack of commitment.
* Storge—Friendship love based on sharing and caring, not passion or excitement.
* Pragma—Logical 'shopping-list' love, realistic but unromantic.
* Agape—All-giving, selfless love, likely to be episodic rather than a constant.
* Mania—Possessive dependant love, anxious and needy, manipulative and deceitful.

Make yourself free to love only in those ways that enrich your brain and soul!

LOOSEN THE POWER OF YOUR INNER CRITIC

None of us leave our childhood behind without gaining an 'Inner Critic' of some sort. This 'sub-personality' lives within us and will 'speak up' uninvited; causing us to doubt our self-worth, criticise many of our behaviours; and even challenge the validity and relevance of our own thoughts. We can tie ourself up in knots trying to please our Inner Critic—which is just a part of us that was created when we were very young, by our 'child-brain'. As such it does not have a valid place in our adult life and it will only sabotage us, in a variety of ways.

We need to dis-empower this Inner Critic and not allow him/her to bully and restrict us any longer.

An effective way to get to know this part of yourself is to:

* Give it a name—preferably a funny one.
* Give it a cartoon-like image.
* Actually ask it what it needs and why it is saying what it says. What is its 'purpose' in your life?
* Thank it for trying to help you to avoid failure and shame, but reassure it that you, as an adult, can now be relied upon to take charge of your own life.

LIFTING THE WEIGHT OF DEPRESSION

There are many causes of depression, both physical and psycho-emotional; and many ways in which depression shows itself.

Our whole body adapts to our emotional state—particularly if it's a chronic and prolonged mood imbalance—and all of our body systems are adversely affected.

If you imagine that when you're depressed your energy is so heavy it is down in your boots—like trying to run with diving boots on. This weight causes your whole body to 'do' depression; and you develop a 'depressed me' posture and persona, which can be harder to shift the longer it is around. Some people have become so attached to this aspect of themselves that they identify with it almost all of the time.

Energetically we need to shift our energy upwards, from our feet and into our legs and bodies.

* Make a list of anything that lifts your mood—even a little bit—such as certain music, certain positive and up-beat people, animals and happy children, nature/scenery, volunteer work, any physical activity you can manage.

* Whenever you are feeling only 4 out of 10 on a happiness scale then ensure that you do one or more of these things—and consciously imagine lifting up the energy from your boots and make the diving boots change into walking boots, then trainers, then slippers.

* Walk, or sit, upright and let the energy rise up your spine and rest in your head like a bright light.

You are what you think, believe, and visualise!

WHY YOU SHOULD BECOME MORE OPTIMISTIC.

Optimism can be learnt, and it is well worth doing so because having an optimistic outlook boosts our levels of happiness and confidence.

Research shows that the optimists among us are more aware that positive outcomes depend upon their own efforts; they don't give up easily, and yet they are also more vigilant of risks and threats.

Being optimistic enables us to look for possible alternatives to a situation as well as to adopt effective ways of dealing with it. Optimists are able to take 'direct action'; they make the best of a bad situation, and they are better able to deal with any health problems, as well as themselves experiencing better overall health than pessimists do. Optimistic women are shown to be less likely to experience post-natal depression.

The way in which we each 'explain' ourself is an indicator of our level of optimism;

A Pessimistic style—"Just my luck...typical of things to go wrong for me...I thought as much"

An Optimistic style—" I have something useful to learn from this....I can cope with this challenge."

If you think that your prospects are bright and that you can overcome adversity, you will feel more energised, motivated and enthusiastic.

So the message is clear..... we need to find out what is restricting our optimism, and work at changing this block to our well-being...... I know you can do it!

<u>Showing A Little Kindness—The Helper's High.</u>

Both showing and receiving kindness makes us feel better, happier and of value.

Helping others leads people to like you (as long as they trust that your motives are honourable), and to appreciate you, and to show their gratitude to you; and perhaps reciprocate the good deed in some way. This is called the 'Helper's High.'

Showing spontaneous acts of kindness to other people, from all walks of life, throughout our everyday lives has an enormous impact upon both the giver and receiver—way beyond the actual act itself, which might only have been a small gesture, offer of assistance, or gift.

Research shows that simply witnessing, or hearing about, an act of kindness leads people to feel 'elevated' and it increases their desire to perform good deeds. This was seen after September 11th tragedy—when the sight of heroic acts and kindness resulted in a 5-fold increase in blood donations as well as generating many charitable acts and groups; and the formation of the Meet-up groups which have now become a worldwide way of meeting 'like-minded' people (see www.meetup.com).

But as a word of caution—don't overdo it or try to help those who don't want or need your help. Some people, because of their own history, may feel hostile in the face of your kindness.

Be kind and your world opens up to more kindness. LIKE ATTRACTS LIKE!

Nurturing Your Real Relationships

In a world of 'virtual' friends and social media sites we can become detached from the give and take of our real physical relationships.

The happier we are, the more likely we are to have a larger circle of friends and companions, a romantic partner and reliable social support. We all like genuinely happy people!

This works both ways—good partners and friendships bring us happiness; and happy people are more likely to find and keep such friends and lovers.

Huge amounts of literature shows that people who are lonely or in unhappy relationships suffer such ill effects as depression, anxiety, jealousy, stress and impaired health.

Scientists tell us that the secrets of successful relationships are:

*Spending time talking, showing an interest in the other and expressing our gratitude.

*Making time for rituals and play—with no TV/PC distractions!

*Showing feelings with a positive to negative ratio of 5:1—for every negative comment there should be 5 positive ones!

*Focussing on the positive attributes that initially attracted you to them; and on the good memories you have.

*Realise what benefits you both get from the relationship.

Our relationships are vital to us—and deserving of our focussed time, attention and care.

TAKING BACK CONTROL OF YOUR ANXIETY AND FEAR

When our anxiety and fear are aroused, then our thinking is subdued. When our brain is focussing on a 'threat'—whether real or imagined—we cannot think, plan, weigh-up consequences, or even express ourselves clearly or effectively. I am assuming here that any such anxiety and fear isn't based upon an immediate life-threatening situation—in such a case you will be thankful for the Adrenalin rushing through your body and preparing you to fight or run!

When in a state of 'alert', our energy is focussed outside of ourselves as we scan for threats; or we may freeze to the spot. Our breathing is shallow and only in the upper part of the chest.

We must then calm down our body and mind by slowing down the breath, and extending the out-going breath. We can then re-focus, and in-turn engage the frontal cortex area of our brain, which changes our experience of events and enables us to think and plan a way through our difficulties.

* Become aware of your body—its posture, and its contact with the ground/chair/bed that you are on.

* Focus on your senses in this moment—what you can see in your peripheral vision as you hold eye contact with one spot? What can you hear, in one minute, as you look at the 'seconds' hand on a clock/watch face, or watch the clouds in the sky?

* Become an 'observer of detail'. Any object nearby will do. Just fully notice everything about it. The colour tones and textures, the smell, the weight…all of the minute details that you would ordinarily ignore.

Our brains are bombarded with 'data' every moment and we can shift our awareness onto some of the things we would usually disregard. As we do so, we change our 'minds'—that is our emotional state, and we improve our ability to function in a calm and grounded way.

BOUNDARIES—WHAT'S OK AND WHAT'S NOT WITH YOU?

Healthy boundaries bring us a feeling of safety and control. We may have difficulty in setting and maintaining boundaries due to our childhood experiences, and we may have encountered people who disregard our preferences and try to push or destroy our boundaries. It can be easier to soften-up a rigid boundary than it is to firm up weak and vague boundaries.

You will have different boundaries with different people, at different times and in different circumstances

Realise that your boundaries around work/sex/money/time alone/agreeing to help someone etc. are flexible and entirely up to you. No-one should try to make you do anything you do not want to do—and any attempt at emotional blackmail or 'guilt-tripping' is disrespectful to you and must be challenged.

When we know ourselves better we can set the boundaries that suit us best. If you do not feel able to assert your boundary with a particular person, don't be rushed or bullied into agreeing to something you may later regret. Ask for 'thinking it over time' and say you will check your diary/give it more thought/get back to them soon with your decision.

In setting your boundaries ask yourself:

*What is OK and what is not OK with me about what is being asked of me?

*What are my body sensations, and intuition/higher wisdom telling me about this request?

*What is my real preference here?

Assertively state your thoughts, feelings and preferences; perhaps offering an alternative if that suits you better.

GOAL SETTING—MAKE IT WORK!

People who strive for something personally significant are far happier than those who don't have strong dreams or aspirations.

The process of working towards a goal is as important to well-being as attaining the goal itself.

No matter what our level of happiness and fulfilment we all have some kind of goal, and these vary as we age.

Having effective and achievable goals is important to our lives and adds meaning, purpose and the 'good stress' of a challenge.

During a time of crisis, commitment to a goal helps us to cope better.

We all have a strong need to 'belong' and pursuing a goal can entail engaging with other people and belonging to a group of people with a shared interest—e.g. a therapy or weight-loss group.

As we develop our social groups, relationships and networks, our levels of happiness increase and we are better able to thrive.

However, for these goals/aims/targets to be of use to you they need to be:

*Personally satisfying.

*Authentic—and completely your choice.

*Focussed on a specific aim, rather than on avoiding something. e.g. To loose 4 lbs, rather than to be slimmer.

*In harmony with any other goals you have set.

*Activity-based.

*Flexible—as you achieve them in small steps, you set the next step towards the final outcome.

WHY SHOULD YOU BE GRATEFUL?

Gratitude is an antidote to negative emotions such as depression, anxiety, loneliness, envy, disappointment, regret and fear.

Research studies show that 'being thankful for what you have' has the following benefits:

*Promotes a 'savouring' of your life's experiences.

*Bolsters self-worth and self-esteem—as you are not focussing on failures and disappointments.

*Increases your ability to cope with stress....after the 9/11 tragedy in New York, gratitude was found to be the second most commonly experienced emotion, after sympathy.

*You are more likely to help others, and less likely to be materialistic.

*Social bonds are strengthened, and new ones more easily formed.

*Envy of others and negative social comparisons are reduced.

*Feelings of anger, greed and bitterness are diminished.

*You are much less likely to take things for granted.

It is recommended that, every evening, you think of at least three things that you have experienced throughout the day that you are grateful for....it may even be for hearing a song you like, or a sunny day. Perhaps you feel grateful for your family, your work, your home, income, life-choices, a good meal, good company, quiet solitude and a time to reflect.

You may even be feeling brave enough to thank someone, verbally or in a letter, and show your appreciation of them.

To receive such a message from another is indeed a blessing!

Is The 'Secret' Not Working For You?

Have you read the books, seen the films, and done all the visualising and cosmic ordering, but to no avail? Join the club!

It is a universal truth (known as the law of coherence and resonance) that we attract that which we give out. We get what we focus upon and we see what we believe we will see. We must not be attached to 'how' the results will come to us. We must, instead live 'as though' we already have that which we seek. We are all responsible for creating our own reality and what it includes.

However, there are other considerations which may be blocking you from receiving that which you have 'ordered'—and are still awaiting—from the Universe.

Your sub-conscious mind has a 'Script' for your life and it will ensure that what you experience on the outside is only ever a reflection of what you have as a core belief on the inside.

Your sub-conscious mind is 'running the show' of your life over 90% of the time. It was predominantly set up in early childhood, and is resistant to change. It cannot be changed by the logical, rational conscious mind or talking therapies alone.

So....if you really want to change the movie that you are staring in—then you'd better learn how to change the script you've been reading from! This involves revising your sub-conscious belief system, which is now do-able.... and that's no secret! (for more information about this process see www.qpp.uk.com)

A Change is as Good as a Rest

We humans all have a need for variety and change—too much and we become stressed, and too little and we become bored. Change is our constant companion. We are most engaged in life when we are challenged—either by our own choice and design, or otherwise. Challenge and change force us to stretch and give more of ourselves. We grow as we learn new things about ourselves and the world. Tackling challenges has resulted in great human accomplishments in the arts, sciences, architecture and technology.

Some people avoid change and challenge because they fear failure, ridicule, disappointment and the negative judgement of others. Instead, we should rise above these minor and usually incorrect fears and welcome the opportunities and rewards that change and challenge can bring. Enjoy being engaged in life, focus upon the journey and not upon the destination. Be alive in the moment and savour it, live it, enjoy it—and celebrate it!

Expect to feel uncomfortable as you step, or jump, outside your familiar and predictable 'comfort zone' of life.....test and develop new skills that will extend this comfort zone!

Set yourself daily, weekly, monthly and yearly challenges that bring you desired change and help you to master your fears.

Ask yourself: 'If I didn't have fear about this challenge/change then I'd..........' ; and then off you go!

VISUALISATIONS

Having the ability to imagine and visualise is a truly priceless gift, with which we can literally change our lives.

Plenty of research now exists to confirm the power of positively focussed visual imagining, when it is persistently repeated. The beneficial effects of visualisation include improved overall health, emotional balance and mental clarity. The more you use visualisation, the better the results will be. Your brain does not know the difference between what is real and that which is vividly imagined with heartfelt emotion. Our higher self, or rather the Matrix that connects us all and from which all is created by us, then sets in motion the means of bringing about our heartfelt and compassionate intentions.

I offer here some brief visualisations for you to use, as and when you wish, with my own heartfelt intention that they serve you well and bring you positive and tangible improvements in your own created reality, the reality of your 'life'.

VIBRANT HEALTH

Begin with your eyes closed, and take a few deep breaths to relax the body—extending the outgoing breath each time.

Imagine yourself (or even better, actually be) standing under a warm shower; as you feel the water running down your body, repeat this phrase, to yourself, "I have vibrant health in every cell of my body".

Imagine the water cleansing each of your trillions of cells, making them bright, vibrant and healthy and washing away any impurities.

You can also extend this to the systems in your body...."My muscles/ bones/ joints/ organs/ nervous system/ endocrine (hormone) system/ my lymphatic system/ my immune system/ my digestive system/ my reproductive system/ my circulatory system/ my respiratory system/ my brain..... is/are vibrantly healthy.

You get what you believe!

Planting Your Intentions

Setting your intentions each day brings you a day of clarity, purpose and achievement.

It is very helpful to use visualisation as part of this process, because it focusses different regions of the brain onto the task, and therefore makes it more effective and likely to succeed.

Early each morning, close your eyes, and take a few deep breaths, extending the outgoing breath each time.

Now imagine you are planting seedlings into a window box.... each seedling being one of your intentions for the day. Plant no more than six—to give them room to grow and to bloom.

Name each one as you plant it, such as.... "this intention for today is to tidy the loft"...or "this intention for today is to sort out my car insurance"....etc.

Imagine too that you now water the seedlings, and that they are left in a sunny and safe place, and so now have the very best chance of blooming.

Those that do bloom (meaning the intention was met that day), will then die off and make way for the intentions of the next day.

Those that do not bloom (because the intention was not met on that day), can be re-watered and allowed to bloom the next day.

Gratitude

Gratitude is considered to be one of our 'higher' values and denotes an awareness of the blessings we do have, and for which we are thankful.

We can connect with this elevated state any time we wish, we only have to remember to do so!

Daily is best, and has been shown to counteract negative emotional states such as depression, anxiety, resentment, frustration, jealousy and envy.

When in a quiet place, close your eyes and slow down your breathing, and extend your outgoing breath. Now imagine yourself surrounded by bubbles which float around you, each one staying within easy touching distance. Inside each bubble is something for which you feel grateful.....it may be your child(ren), your partner/spouse, your health, the sunny day, the flowers you have received...in fact anything at all that has lifted your spirits.

Watch these bubbles float around you, radiating their rainbow spectrum as they catch the sunlight.

Enjoy the experience and amplify your gratitude for all the awesome things that you do have every day of your life.

Abundant Wealth

Simply wanting financial freedom, security and abundance will not bring it to you. We need to employ all the skills at our disposal. We must have a plan and then take action on it. A very important addition to this pragmatic approach is to include clear and repeated visualisation too.

Find a quiet time and place, close your eyes, take a few deep breaths—extending the outgoing breath; now imagine yourself sitting amidst a large mound of money made up of bright red £50 notes. Play around with the money, scooping it up and letting it 'rain' over you. Actually move your arms and hands as you do this.

Feel 'delighted' to have this money; and feel 'relieved' at what it will bring you, and the choices you can now make in your life by having this financial freedom, security, and abundant wealth. You 'know' that you own all of this money; you are 'confident' that you can have as much as you desire, you feel 'self-assured' because you have 'earned' it, and you 'deserve' it.

Notice any resistance to this image that you experience; which may be your sub-conscious beliefs about your relationship with wealth, and what you deserve in your life.

Such deep rooted beliefs will sabotage your success unless you clear them away. This visualisation will at least expose such resistance that you hold about wealth and financial success.

DIGNITY

Dignity is a little-used word nowadays, but nevertheless it has a huge significance to how we feel about ourselves. Do you live with dignity in your life? Do you walk with dignity? Are you dignified in your dealings with others?

This is not about pride or arrogance, but a calm confident and uplifting sense of your own dignity.

Visualisation can help us to connect with our own dignity, and our bodies can 'experience' this dignity and absorb the higher feeling this brings.

Find a quiet place, and close your eyes. Take a few deep breaths and extend the outgoing breath each time.

Now imagine yourself sitting, or standing, with 'Dignity'. Repeat the word silently to yourself. Imagine a golden cord extending from the top of your spine up beyond your head and high into the sky, and up into the universal energy beyond. Feel your body gently straightened and slightly lifted as you breath in this calming sense of your own inner dignity.

You are always connected, by this golden cord, to your higher self and higher values; and you can remind yourself of this every time you use this visualisation.

Giving Yourself Love and Compassion

We usually find it much easier to offer, and to show, love and compassion to someone else, than we do to ourselves. We can, and should, at least give ourselves these valuable gifts. Compassion is the universal language of creation, and of connection with the Matrix, or web of higher intelligence, within and around us all.

With your eyes closed, take a few deep breaths, extending the outgoing breath. See an image of yourself reflected in a full-length mirror. Notice your posture, facial expression, hair and clothing, without any judgement of what you see. Now imagine slowly approaching this reflection of yourself, and see both of you alongside one another in the mirror, then turn around to become face-to-face, and both hold hands.

Allow yourself to become soft and yielding as you open your heart and project the love and compassion that has always been residing there. Bring that feeling up to your face and particularly to your eyes as you make loving eye contact with yourself. Feel that transfer of love and the compassion for your struggle and progress so far. Magnify that loving compassion until it fills you both up and radiates out to form a glow around you both, holding you safely within it. You know now that your higher self will always be accompanying you on every stage of your life's journey. You are safe and loved just for being who you are.

Changing Stress

Visualisation can be a very helpful method of coping with your levels of stress, because it affects your autonomic nervous system, and activates the Para-sympathetic branch—which calms and soothes you.

Start by finding a quiet place, and close your eyes. Breath deeply and slowly a few times, and extend the outgoing breath.

Take your awareness to your body and locate the place in your body where you are holding your stress. See it as a particular shape, texture and colour. Now imagine reaching into your own body and taking this stress outside of you, and hold it cupped in both hands in front of your body. As you breath, imagine that each outgoing breath changes this object that you are holding and looking at. See the colour gradually become lighter, and see the texture become smoother, and more even. Feel the object become less heavy and dense. Enjoy the changes you experience. After a while gently place the transformed object back inside you into the place that you took it from. Notice how much different you now feel due to the changes that you have made.

Fantasy Collage

As most people are now aware, what you believe is what you get. We need to vividly imagine, experience and fully expect our wishes and desires to materialise, before they have the energy to do so.

Creating your own 'fantasy collage' can be a really useful way of capturing what it is that you are wanting to bring into your life—and with a collage you can include several things at the same time.

Imagine you have a clear canvas upon which you will stick various pictures, drawings and other snippets of what you want in your near future.

You can make the most important subjects larger in size and give them the prominent centre position on the canvas. Notice them in vivid detail and evoke your emotional responses to having them in your life right now.

The act of selecting and positioning is rewarding in itself, and further benefits come with regularly looking at this collage, and perhaps moving things about as you see fit. Just hold the strong desire for these things on your imaginary board/canvas, and watch them change from being your fantasy to becoming your reality!

COURAGE, TENACITY, RESILIENCE AND DETERMINATION

These are the qualities that enable you to carry on despite the challenges and obstacles that threaten to knock you off your chosen path.

Each word represents an aspect of your inner strength and may have been overlooked or hidden in your life so far.

We all need a strong sense of our own identity, presence and power to make a positive difference in the world—and to feel that we matter! These four qualities will help you to do just that.

In a quiet, undisturbed place close your eyes and take a few slow deep breaths, extending the outgoing breath as your body and brain relax into the state which is most influenced by your visualisations.

Now see yourself in any recent situation where you may have lacked these four attributes.....be back there and recall the event as a snapshot or photograph.

You can now imagine altering the image as if using the latest computer technology...and make changes to your facial expression, your body language, and of course your actions—all of which will now be showing you as being courageous, tenacious, resilient and determined to achieve your desired and preferred outcome. Become that expression of courage....be tenacious and unwilling to quit.... be resilient and able to weather the storm....be determined in your actions.

As you see and experience the overall change in the picture snapshot, soak up the new feelings of inner strength and allow them to encircle you and to be fully absorbed by you. You are now capable of showing your courage, tenacity, resilience and determination every day, and to reap the benefits of your more vibrant, energised and effective self.

DISENTANGLEMENT

We become emotionally attached and entangled with other people when we spend our time with them, and it can take us a while to work out that someone is not good for us to be around. Perhaps they drain our energy with their needs, demands or manipulations; maybe they give out negative feelings with their gossip, lies, judgements, sarcasm or put-downs. Even though we may have chosen not to see them any longer or even to keep in touch with them, we may still need to emotionally disengage or disentangle ourself from them. Or it may be that a particular environment, such as a former school, workplace or social venue holds bad memories for you because of bad experiences you had there, and you want to become more detached from it. Visualisation can help to do this.

In a quiet place, close your eyes, and slow down your breathing and extend your outgoing breath. Now bring the person or place to mind—but put them inside a big bubble, which now separates them from you and they cannot impact upon you in the same way ever again As you breath out imagine you are blowing the bubble away from you, and you see it floating up higher and higher, further and further away from you; you see the bubble getting smaller and smaller. Soon you can hardly see it any longer and just as it is almost out of sight you see it burst and it is blown away by the wind, taking the person/place with it. You now feel the lightness and freedom of not having this in your life any longer, you are emotionally separated and no longer entangled with it. Soak up this new lighter feeling, and be strong in knowing that you have the power to cast out any other negative people or places whenever you want to do so.

PEACE

A sense of peace is what we all ultimately want and seek, but many things get in the way of this. We know that as individuals we can ripple out our feelings into the world where they influence other people, and we can choose these feelings to be positive, benevolent, loving, compassionate and peaceful ones. It only takes less than one per cent of the world's population to make a shift and to change the way in which we all live and behave—and visualising peace is a great place to focus our intent. We all need and want peace in our lives, and it starts with each one of us knowing and believing that we can make a difference.

As before, find a quiet undisturbed place, and close your eyes. Slow down your breathing rate and extend your outgoing breath.

Now focus your attention upon the word 'peace' and what it means to you.....enlarge and expand this feeling until in envelops you and you are immersed in it.....feel it lighten every cell in your body.....cleansing and clearing away any impurities or blockages to this feeling of peace, as you gain a sense of complete one-ness with everything that is. This brings you a state of bliss and your brain releases a cascade of feel-good chemicals into every cell of your body. Magnify this wonderful feeling and radiate it out from yourself and into the room, to your town or city, to the country, out further still to the continent ......and as far as the whole of the world....to all people of all colours creeds and beliefs.....Peace be with us all.

MATRIX ORIGAMI

At last there are reputable scientific studies which show the presence of a matrix of connecting consciousness between all things.

We all have the ability to co-create our reality—we just haven't realised it before. Many things get in the way of our believing that we can shape our own lives and we become wrongly convinced that life just happens to us and that we are either its victim, or pawns in its game.

Our own childhood conditioning and subsequent sub-conscious belief system—which was created from and is sustained by our own fears (an example of our ability to create our own life situation)—trick us into feelings of passivity, helplessness and even hopelessness for some.

We can reconnect with the Matrix by using our will-power and our heartfelt emotions. We can turn our dominant thoughts and repeated visualisations into our new reality—with persistence and faith.

With your eyes closed, slow down your breathing, and as before, extend your outgoing breaths. When your body and mind have slipped into a calm and relaxed state, imagine a mesh made of vivid criss-crossed light. This mesh envelops you, and stretches out to cover the room you are in, the building, the county, the country, the world and far into space. It is all there is and you realise that you are created from this mesh-like energy, like a wrinkle or a pucker in a cloth, or a ripple on a calm pond. As you watch this Matrix slowly and rhythmically vibrate you notice other such shifts in the light-mesh which then form themselves into other people, trees, birds, mountains and all of what makes up the planet as you usually see it.

You can choose to create anything you deeply desire from this matrix—like an intricate origami creation without the two-dimensional paper. Your strong thoughts, images and desires become the folds which then form into your newly created reality

Consider the life you want to create from the Matrix of ultimate creativity—now that you finally realise that you have the innate power to do so.

You do not have to remain ignorant of this power—you can become an Matrix Origami master, with practice and persistence.

৸ ৸ ৸

If you would like to attend any of the 12 Psycho-Emotional-Educational modules of 'The Ripple Effect' Process please see the Licensee page on the website www.the-ripple-effect.co.uk **for contact details of the licensee closest to you.**

If you want or be considered as a prospective licensee to present the modules to the public in your area then please contact me by e-mail at office@the-ripple-effect.co.uk

(Note: Licensee must have a reputable counselling qualification and their own private practice, and professional insurance.)

To change your sub-conscious belief system please see Quantum Psyche Process and www.qpp.uk.com

NAMASTE

About the Author

Maxine Harley (Msc Integrative Psychotherapy) has almost 20 years of clinical experience and has identified the gaps in what counselling, psychotherapy and coaching services have to offer. She has created 'The Ripple Effect' Process to fill these gaps.

She lives in West Sussex, England, and has a daughter and grandson—from whom she has learned the most.

Lightning Source UK Ltd.
Milton Keynes UK
UKOW042131170912

199171UK00001B/45/P

9 781452 556642